The Book of Comic Prayer

Using Art and Humor to Transform Youth Ministry

The Book of Comic Prayer

Using Art and Humor to Transform Youth Ministry

HEATHER J. ANNIS

Morehouse Publishing
NEW YORK

Unless otherwise noted, the Scripture quotations contained herein are from the New Revised Standard Version Bible, copyright © 1989 by the Division of Christian Education of the National Council of Churches of Christ in the U.S.A. Used by permission. All rights reserved.

Images and Comics used by permission:
Sam © Ike Maness
Phil the Gill, The Lord's Prayer Rebus, Pew Potatoes, Mike,
 and The Carnivorous Bongo Brothers © Brian Materne
Super Chalice, Wonder Wafer, and *Holy Molar* © Wendy Foley
Mr. Peace Flag © Ben Geoghegan
Blur, Prayer Press, and *Explanation Point* © Gabrielle S.
Derpy and *Fess* © Laughlin Billingsley
The Lollipop Dragon, Rita, and *Spike* © Tessa Foley
Mr. Peace, Jedediah, Daily Brains, and *Abby's Panel* © Abigail Ray
All other images © Heather J. Annis

Morehouse Publishing, 19 East 34th Street, New York, NY 10016

Morehouse Publishing is an imprint of Church Publishing Incorporated.
www.churchpublishing.org

Cover art by Heather J. Annis
Cover design by Laurie Klein Westhafer, Bounce Design
Typeset by Beth Oberholtzer

Library of Congress Cataloging-in-Publication Data
A catalog record of this book is available from the Library of Congress.

ISBN-13: 978-0-8192-3278-6 (pbk)
ISBN-13: 978-0-8192-3279-3 (ebook)

Printed in the United States of America

Contents

Acknowledgments

I would like to thank everyone who helped make this project a reality:

The members of the St. John's youth group—especially the Art Team—for their creativity, enthusiasm, dedication, and hard work;

Pat Hines for instilling in me a love of writing and doggedness for producing quality work;

Marilyn Sanders and Wendy Foley, for their kind words of support throughout this process;

My editor, Sharon Ely Pearson, for her wisdom, patience, and advice every step of the way;

The fine people at the Time Capsule and Mycomicshop .com for helping me to find and obtain obscure and surprising resources;

The Center for Cartoon Studies for their generosity in allowing me to access the materials at the Schulz Library;

Erica DeCoste and Jackie Rogers for recognizing and encouraging my interest in cartooning in junior high and high school (and for letting me doodle in class!);

And to my partner, Kelly, for allowing me to take over the dining room table with piles of books, comics, notes, and binders.

Introduction

> Lord, teach us to pray.
>
> —Luke 11:1

Walk into any Episcopal church and you will very likely encounter rows of pews or chairs dotted with red books. Pick up one of these volumes and you will see that the middle section is worn and tattered from use. The Book of Common Prayer is the foundation upon which Episcopalians structure prayer and worship. Our catechism defines prayer as "responding to God, by thought and by deeds, with or without words."[1] Theologian John Westerhoff defines prayer as "anything we do that enhances and enlivens our relationship with God."[2] These are the working definitions that drive the stories, observations, instructions, and suggestions in the following pages.

As I write these words, the 78th General Convention of the Episcopal Church has just ended in Salt Lake City. One of the convention's resolutions is "to prepare a plan for the comprehensive revision" of the current Book of Common Prayer.[3] Since the convention, the resolution has been met with both enthusiasm and apprehension. Fiddling with the gold standard of Anglican prayer is a topic charged with history and emotion. It begs uncomfortable questions about a subject that is, itself, often uncomfortable. What is prayer for? What does it look like? Am I doing it right? Will changing the words of the prayers to which we are accustomed fundamentally change the way we pray?

These questions are quite similar to the questions the young people I minister with are addressing in their work with art and comics; they have already begun the work of adapting the prayer book to meet their needs. C.S. Lewis expressed concern about the changes to the 1928 prayer book when they were proposed and subsequently adopted in the 1979, but conceded that the idea of a timeless vocabulary of prayer and worship is "nonsense."[4] The vernacular of liturgy changes, often depending on context and audience. These changes are especially pertinent to our youth, who have grown up learning certain words and phraseologies that are often both familiar and comforting as well as incomprehensible and unwieldy. Using art and humor to navigate through the context and vocabulary of individual and corporate prayer can be educational and entertaining.

When art and humor combine to form comics, the results can lead to imaginative dialogue between church and culture. *The Book of Comic Prayer* explores this opportunity through interactive, experiential, and spirit-driven exercises designed to engage young people in conversation about and in the act of prayer.

The disciples asked Jesus to teach them to pray. Our youth group asked us to teach them, and proceeded to teach us how it is that *they* pray. They pray with thought and actions, with words, drawings, photographs, poetry, and a sense of humor that can do no less than to enliven and enrich their relationships with God.

Let us pray.

CHAPTER 1

Origin Stories

Art, Comics, and Youth Ministry

> If you do not say anything in a cartoon, you might as well not draw it at all.
>
> —*Charles Schulz*[5]

I drew my first "religious" comic strip when I was nine or ten years old. Drawn in pencil on a narrow piece of poster board, it is called "The Three Wise Dudes" and is about the magi journeying toward Bethlehem. The camels are too slow, so the three supposedly wise men trade them in for a dune buggy. The beaming kings whiz across the desert sands, holding their crowns on with their hands. The dune buggy soon gets a flat tire, at which point the grumbling wise dudes end up back on the camels.

I drew the cartoon because I thought it was funny. I'm not sure I appreciated the irony, or that this was really a strip about patience: the patience of the journey from Advent to Christmas, from Christmas to Epiphany. Neither did I identify the crude drawings as prayer or commentary. Years later, I realized that I had something to say and could say it with comics.

As a kid, I scrawled pictures of Woody Woodpecker, Snoopy, and Donald Duck over every available surface. Since then, I have created a number of comics about a super-heroic sock, a little girl named Pentimento Jones, a robotic creature called Mobie, and, among other things, my work with teenagers.

The middle school and high school kids with whom I have worked over the years have personalities and stories as varied as cartoon characters. In each case, I have found the arts to be a logical and gratifying

Heather J. Annis

entry point into difficult topics. As an artist, comic book fan, and Christian educator, it makes sense that these three elements of my vocational identity should come together to influence and shape my ministry.

For the past several years, I have also been traveling around the country doing workshops and presentations on the subject of art and faith. Jon Bowles suggests, "The church needs artists to come out from the margins and actively lead in the spiritual formation of its people."[6] The Book of Common Prayer affirms this sentiment by its inclusion of a little-known prayer for church artists and musicians:

> O God, whom saints and angels delight to worship in heaven:
> Be ever present with your servants who seek through art and
> music to perfect the praises offered by your people on earth; and
> grant to them even now glimpses of your beauty and make them
> worthy at length to behold it unveiled for evermore; through
> Jesus Christ our Lord. *Amen.*[7]

Participants in my workshops are unfailingly surprised and delighted by the inclusion of this prayer. Its existence is evidence of the importance of the arts in all their forms to the religious community.

Most faith traditions have made room for visual reminders of God's presence in worship and personal devotion. Christians have long made use of icons, mosaics, and stained glass to communicate a sense of the holy. Islamic calligraphy is highly regarded as the embodiment of the sacred word. Making art to focus attention, direct prayer, and articulate the commandments is a component of Jewish worship. Buddhists and Native Americans create mandalas and sand paintings for the glorification of deities, healing of the community, and out of reverence for the earth.

The potency of art as a spiritual discipline lies in its ability to evoke and make known the presence of the divine. In addition to aesthetic functions, the arts have played a historical role in Christian education. Certainly the arts have been employed as tools of instruction throughout the history of the Church. One need only turn to stained glass windows and illuminated texts for evidence of the role visual arts have played in promoting the faith over the centuries. The illustrations that accompany early Christian manuscripts served to deepen religious understanding by making it accessible to a largely illiterate society. Early iconographers, illuminators, and mosaicists sought ways to enter into visual dialogue with God.

The visual arts can enliven one's search for God when used as or in conjunction with worship, prayer, and study. There is no shortage of precedent for pairing word and image, ancient and modern; the drawings and stories in this book provide continued evidence of the place of these arts within Christian formation and spiritual practice.

Participatory Aesthetics

My particular interest in the arts and ministry falls into the category of participatory aesthetics—really a fancy way of saying "making art together." Participatory aesthetics asks how worship spaces, spiritual practices, and religious encounters can be mediated and enhanced by communal engagement in the arts. Two fundamental assumptions of this approach are that "all the gifts and abilities that individuals possess are from God and, if surrendered to God, can become vehicles for

spiritual ministry" and that these gifts can be used for "the perpetu-
ation of community life."[8] Furthermore, the work of Leonard Sweet
contends that in the post-modern age, the American religious institu-
tion is in need of a re-imagining of both worship and education. His
"E.P.I.C." model of church life advocates a shift toward a more active,
community-oriented style of religious engagement, suggesting that this
engagement ought to be Experiential, Participatory, Image-driven, and
Connected. He asserts that post-modern churchgoers are interested in
helping to create what they experience.[9] It stands to reason, then, that
the interconnected processes of prayer, education, and discernment
can be enriched through the thoughtful use of the arts.

   With these historical and philosophical underpinnings in mind,
I have made it my vocation to explore the symbiotic relationships
among art, faith, and community. As a youth minister and arts con-
sultant, I have facilitated community projects from wall-sized murals
to comics you can fit into the pocket of your jeans. While the practical considerations differ significantly, the approach is essentially the
same: value the gifts and contributions of each individual, using them
to build relationships, enrich faith, and glorify God.

Comics in Community

In his book on arts ministry, Michael Bauer states that creativity is
"the result of openness to new ways of thinking, new approaches to
solving problems, new materials, new paradigms."[10] As professor of
Christian education Robert Pazmiño observes, "an educational program that gives participants the opportunity to express their creativity
will also foster a sense of celebration and provide occasions for worship."[11] These statements are crucial to an understanding of how the
arts in general function within the context of spiritual formation. How
the use of comics, in particular, fits into this model requires a bit more
background and exploration.

   According to comics and graphic novel legend Will Eisner, comics can serve two basic functions: to instruct and/or to entertain.
The combination of words and images can be used to communicate
shared experience and to provide new information. This assumption
is at the core of visual literacy, a concept that is of particular value

and significance in the increasingly image-saturated culture in which we live and to which Sweet's "E.P.I.C." model alludes. "To be visually literate," maintains Lynell Burmark, students must be able to both consume and produce "visually rich communications. They must be able to move gracefully and fluently between text and images, between literal and figurative worlds."[12] In comics and graphic novels, it is easy for both artist and reader to "make the move from the realistic to the fantastic . . . it can be done from one panel to the next or even within one panel. We accept strange transformations in comics."[13] The same delicate balance is necessary to be spiritually literate: this ability to negotiate the worlds of religious tradition and story–from fact to metaphor to experience. The ability to situate oneself prayerfully within this tension can be nurtured through creating a form of art, which, by its very nature, is a juxtaposition of revelation and implied meaning.

Finding meaning in the blank spaces between comic panels, or gutters, requires a certain participatory leap, an act of both imagination and faith. Finding God in the blank spaces between prayers–sometimes even in the midst of prayer itself–can be challenging and frustrating. Encouraging students to engage in prayer as an act of imaginative interactivity is of both creative and spiritual value.

Like prayer, the comics are at once deceptively simple and complex. While there is no "right way" to pray, there are forms and compositional structures that can make the process less frustrating. Similarly, "when students learn the composing techniques associated with the comics form, they tell compelling stories that often connect to [their] lived experiences and actual social worlds, rather than to capes and tights."[14] That is to say, while drawings may initially seem superficial, the comics and prayers that students generate offer rich glimpses into the spiritual environment of the teenaged heart, mind, and soul.

Re-Envisioning the Three Rs

Within the context of youth ministry, comics offer a new interpretation of the three Rs: reach, relevance, and relationship. Each of these attributes alone constitutes a reason for exploring comics with youth. Together, they make a compelling argument for incorporating comics into your programming.

Reach

In a strip called *Mish and Meedja,* a priest and a missionary stroll down a busy street. They are virtually surrounded by comics: on racks at a newsstand, in a vending machine, in a shop selling books and magazines. The other people in the strip are engrossed in comic books as the two clergy people walk by. "I give up!" moans the pastor. "I just can't find a way to reach these people!"[15] Far from giving up, the Church is called to identify and embrace new mediums for exploration and expression in education, formation, and evangelism.

Comic books, manga, and graphic novels are becoming increasingly popular in the United States; indeed, the medium of sequential art has its own subculture. Over 125,000 people attended the San Diego Comic-Con in 2014.[16] Libraries have begun to pay attention to this literary trend by supplementing their holdings with books of sequential art popular with teens.

For an admittedly apples to oranges (but useful) comparison: *The Economist* estimates that more than a hundred million Bibles are printed every year,[17] making a staggering total of over six billion in print.[18] According to Diamond Comic Distributors (responsible for the direct market distribution of Marvel, DC, Dark Horse, IDW, and Image comics in the United States), their top ten titles sold over one million copies in the month of April 2015 alone. Fourth-ranked *Batman* sold an estimated 131,128 copies in that same month.[19]

The influence of comic book and cartoon characters is extensive. Character movies, toys, and other merchandise are pervasive in American culture, and the effects of their prevalence begin at an early age. Marketing and packaging matter; studies show that advertising with cartoon characters, for example, plays a strong role in inducing children and youth to consume products and engage in behaviors. What if we were able and willing to make prayer and worship more appealing to young people, thus attracting them to both spiritual practice and organized religion without changing the fundamental qualities of each?

Other organizations figured this out long ago. Thirty years ago, the comic book became a popular medium through which to deliver public service announcements sponsored by government and non-profit agencies to promote everything from good nutrition and dental hygiene to preventing smoking and drug use. As recently as 2013,

Spider-Man and the Fantastic Four teamed up to battle underage drinking. In 2014, more than thirty cartoonists and comic writers contributed to a book dedicated to the prevention of bullying.

For the Church's part, Christian-themed comics and graphic novels are slowly increasing in number, quality, variety, availability, and popularity. Done well, a comic book treatment of a religious message can be an invaluable resource for evangelism and education. The fundamentalist comic booklets known as "Chick tracts" offer over one hundred titles, translated into more than one hundred languages, sold by the bundle. Remember those figures about the production of Bibles and comic books? Jack Chick sells an estimated half-billion copies of conservative comics each year[20] and according to a letter from Chick Publications, the company has mailed out nearly "900 million tracts worldwide"[21] in the past fifty years. Agree or disagree with their ideology, the tracts are high quality and they sell; if nothing else, we can take a lesson from their marketing strategy. As Robert Short observes, "the popular arts are important precisely because they are popular."[22] Which brings us to the topic of relevance.

Relevance

Pastor and author Rob Bell urges the church to find fresh, new ways to approach formation, saying "every generation has to ask the difficult questions of what it means to be a Christian here and now, in this place, in this time."[23] Part of the Church's task is to engage with popular culture, reclaiming tradition in ways that both respect history and evolve to make room for new meaning. The telling of stories has always been a cornerstone of religious tradition, providing a means of transmitting information, values, and experience. Sequential art frames stories within a structure that is flexible yet clear, offering what Darby Orcutt calls a "natural fit between comics and religious narrative."[24] Sequential art, therefore, is an apt choice for telling stories, especially stories that promote religious history, function, and values.

This being the case, the art of the comic carries with it not only cultural and religious relevance, but a responsibility by consumers to be critical thinkers, parsing out what is significant and why. Superheroes and comics are relevant because they represent regular people with the same passions and worries as the rest of us. The comics provide both social commentary and a vehicle through which to express our lives as ordinary people with heroic potential.

The idea that comics have something important to say about prayer (or even *as* prayer) may seem itself outrageous. But, like most art and literary forms, comics afford a way to challenge and fulfill the assumption that prayer is all around us all the time, through intention, practice, and openness to the Holy Spirit. Prayer is authentic and personal; good comics have elements of universal truth and autobiography. Comics can shape our beliefs just as beliefs give shape to the comic art form. Telling our stories in word and picture is unquestionably relevant; and saying our prayers is foundational to who we are as God's people. Putting the two modalities together connects private devotions with corporate worship, making prayer personal, communal, and visible. In visibility, there is the potential for relationship.

Relationship

John Westerhoff notes, "We often forget that prayer is the means by which we become aware of what God would like us to do *together*."[25] Creating comics together requires teamwork, attention to detail, critical thinking, and a willingness to try out the new ways of thinking, materials, problem solving, and paradigms to which Michael Bauer refers. Each quality of Bauer's creative leap contributes to learning and fostering relationships:

- **Thinking:** One of the hallmarks of a group comic (or any art project in which community input is desired) is brainstorming. Understanding the basic "rules" of the brainstorming process often requires an adjustment in how we think. In brainstorming, we cultivate the outrageous. We listen. We accept everyone's ideas as valuable and worth considering, even as we make decisions about which ideas to use and which to set aside. In addition, the inherent characteristics of comics necessitate a sort of truncated method of storytelling. One must think in boxes and word balloons, from another's point of view, and allow the improbable to be possible.

- **Materials:** In our art team cabinet, we keep a bin of basic comics-creating equipment: mechanical pencils, white erasers, black flair pens, tracing paper, sketchbooks, colored pencils, and scissors.

Most of these materials are familiar to kids, but some require explanation and instruction. The same goes for learning new software such as Photoshop, Manga Studio, or ComicLife. Each student also receives a notebook in which to record his or her ideas and quick sketches. They often share what they have written with the group to get feedback and advice. They talk with each other to determine which gags are funny, what the shape of a character's eyes should be, and how to fill in gaps in their storylines. While they are doing their own individual drawings, these drawings are part of a larger project, so conversation is vital in ensuring that the project both showcases individual ideas and talents while making sense as a coherent whole.

- **Problem solving:** The ways in which word balloons, characters, panels, and gutters function are really exercises in problem solving. The cartoonist needs to make decisions about what to put in and what to leave to the reader's imagination in order for continuity to exist. Furthermore, integrating students of differing interests and abilities causes them to work together. If one kid has a shaky hand, another steps in to help make clean lines. This requires not only a steady hand, but also trust.

- **Paradigms:** Shifting ways of thinking actually builds relationships when the shift occurs in a group. It causes kids to ask questions: What if prayer were relevant to us? What if prayer could be funny? What if we really do have something to say about prayer? The Book of Common Prayer provides a set of rubrics for communal prayer.[26] Making prayers in comic strip format requires modifying the established system of prayer, a system within which most of my youth group members have grown up.

Producing a comic book requires working in close quarters with deadlines, distilling the ideas of a large group into something that represents that group while having continuity of text and image, compromising, and sharing thoughts with each other as well as the larger audience. Encountering materials with which they are unfamiliar, like non-photo blue pencils or transfer paper, offers kids an opportunity to explore and learn new skills in the context of a church group.

Calvin and Hobbes pokes fun at the comic book industry's use of multiple artists and writers. "Look at the committee that drew this issue," Calvin exclaims.[27] True, a Marvel or DC comic book can employ as many as a half-dozen people on a single issue, including writers, pencillers, inkers, and colorists. It is a rough parallel to the illuminated prayer books and other manuscripts of the Middle Ages. For the monks who created these treasures, it was a group effort undertaken by craftspeople, scribes, artists, gilders, and bookbinders. For the modern self-published comic, a similar blend of teamwork and division of labor exists—some draw, others write, some outline, and others copy, fold, and staple the finished product.

Relationship grows not just within the group creating the comic, but extends outward into the congregation and larger community. In our youth group's case, we found that our older youth were forming relationships and having conversations with both younger and older members. Pierce, then a third-grader, has been very keen on following the youth group's progress. When it comes time for the group to sell the finished product, he eagerly volunteers to parade around the coffee hour wearing a sandwich board and peddling comics. He has turned out to be our best salesperson and remains eager to be a sixth-grader so he, too, can join the youth group.

Further conversation with parishioners and visitors—including the bishop—was generated following a sermon detailing the comics' process and philosophy. Youth group members wrote and delivered the sermon and were available after the service to chat. Finally, the relationships between leaders and group members are a natural by-product of most creative undertakings. Becoming comfortable with their ability to express themselves visually and verbally, the kids also became more comfortable talking about prayer along with its benefits and challenges. In addition to the pride and accomplishment they displayed with the completed comic book, they have become a solid working team and are gaining respect as representatives of their church community.

New Translations: About the Terms Used in This Book

For loose definitions of basic comic vocabulary, I've included an excerpt from Dan Clanton's chapter on the subject. I will often use the term "cartoon" to refer to animated cartoons as well as to Clanton's definition:

> The cartoon is a single panel work that delivers to the viewer one static scene. Because of its form, it lacks substance and elaboration and instead relies on inherited and recognizable images and conventions . . . to convey its message . . . As such, a cartoon is different from a comic strip, which is usually characterized as "sequential art," that is, a piece containing several panels that tell a more intricate story or joke. Furthermore, the "comic book" is a term that usually refers to a serialized piece of sequential art, often with more detail and depth of plot than a newspaper comic strip. Finally, there is the graphic novel, which can be a collection of comic books or simply a novel told in the form of text and images.[28]

For the sake of convenience, I will often use the term "comics" to refer to all types of sequential art. With this broad usage comes the understanding that different types of comics will lend themselves to different applications. As with faith, it is the nature of the comic medium to be structured, yet flexible. Vocabulary aside, comics present opportunities to be both amusing and deeply meaningful.

So, if you have something to say to God or about God, you might as well draw it.

CHAPTER 2

Drawing Closer to God

Art as Prayer

> Art is prayer made visible.

—*The Reverend Gina Rose Halpern*[29]

The title of this chapter is a shameless interpretation of James 4:8: "Draw near to God and he will draw near to you." This passage is not really about the act of drawing, but about inviting God into our lives by being open, present, and proactive. That said, I would argue that making art–whether painting, dancing, music, poetry, comics, or any other form–provides unique opportunities to enter into relationship with the divine.

When I was four years old, I created my first overtly religious drawing. Neatly labeled by my mother for clarification, the drawing consists of a large triangular gentleman with purple hair, smoking a pipe: "Jesus." The figure identified as "God" is a squat green-eared fellow hovering in mid-air wearing a hat that closely resembles a garbage can lid. Also included are Mary, a sun, and a lamb. While I have no recollection of making this drawing, I suspect that it was an early attempt to connect with God using the tools I had at my disposal: a box of crayons and a desire for that connection. I believe this brittle and yellowing piece of paper represents prayer in all its innocence and purity. And I believe this type of prayer is available through the arts regardless of age, ability, or religious persuasion.

Artist Isaac Brynjegard-Bialik is a master at finding connections between prayer and the comics. He "combines traditional papercutting techniques with collage to create intricate pieces whose inspirations span centuries, blurring the lines between graphic storytelling and decorative arts, pop culture and worship."³⁰ One piece, entitled "Barchu," is a visual representation of a prayer characterized by community participation. The artist writes, "The Barchu marks the beginning of the formal prayer service, the moment when we stop being just a group of individuals and become a community praying together."³¹

Comic books and strips are readily available, cheap to purchase and produce, and, if you look closely, have much to say about religion, prayer, and worship.

Precedent and Practice

As Brynjegard-Bialik demonstrates, art can be both about prayer and the prayer itself. One focuses on the product while the other focuses on the process. In comic prayer, the focus is on both process and product simultaneously. As seen in the illuminated Bibles and Psalters of the Middle Ages, as well as icons used in Orthodox practice, the pairing of art and prayer is an ancient device with contemporary application.

I have witnessed the value of connecting art and prayer in countless classes and workshops, especially with young people who can be squirrelly about calling prayer "prayer." I have watched kids give shape to prayers using googly eyes, silly outfits, and talking animals. These characters and traits personify a playful approach to an enterprise often seen as reserved for the pious. As we will see in chapter 3, playfulness and piety are not mutually exclusive.

The act of praying has been depicted in countless paintings, illuminations, sculptures, and other art forms for centuries. Using art *as* prayer or for the mediation thereof is not a new concept, but I would venture to say that, at least within the Anglican tradition, creativity in prayer is not high on the list of liturgical or educational priorities. Rubrics and self-consciousness distract us; kids are the first to pick up on this behavior and when they do, prayer immediately loses some of its richness and personality.

C.S. Lewis alludes to this personality of prayer in *Letters to Malcolm*, referring to the "private overtones" he gives to prayers as "festoons." This labeling reflects the importance of rote and ritual while honoring the individualized nature of even communal prayer. Festoons, he says, do not "obliterate the plain, public sense of the petition but are merely hung on it."[32]

This characterization captures the very essence of the value of the arts in teaching, learning, and experiencing the practice of prayer in its many forms. Art–from music and dance to poetry and painting–is the festoon that, when hung upon the Lord's Prayer, the Nicene Creed, or the confession, transforms that prayer into something dynamic. Googly eyes, silly outfits, and talking animals are festoons that can enable children and youth to engage with prayer, to engage with sacred texts, to engage with God in a language that is uniquely their own, yet shared in community. Whereas the study of prayer requires intellect, the act of prayer requires imagination.[33] Study and imagination are essential to an effective formation program and it is this fusion that will be the focus of subsequent chapters.

CHAPTER 3

Sunday Funnies

Humor in Prayer and Worship

> Humor is the prelude to faith, and laughter is the beginning of prayer.
>
> —Reinhold Niebuhr[34]

For many people of faith, Sunday mornings are about ritual. When I was a child, church-going was the central Sunday morning ritual: riding in the back seat of our green station wagon, passing through four towns and over the Mount Hope Bridge before arriving at a small white church with the ubiquitous red door. Inside were the sights, scents, sounds, and textures that I came to associate with prayer and worship: the maroon carpet that held the scents of candle smoke, spice, and dust; organ pipes, guitar strings, and the occasional clanking of the tambourine; the well-worn prayer books with the middle section of pages falling out. Here I absorbed the poetry of the collects, canticles, and the Great Thanksgiving. Here I learned about silence and celebration, about laughing and crying and praying in community.

Another ritual awaited me upon our return home. The *Providence Sunday Journal* arrived on our front porch every week, a heavy parcel smelling of newsprint and ink. After church, we would adjourn to the living room, where my mother clipped coupons and puffed on cheap cigarettes. My father sipped his coffee and studied the business section. My bailiwick was the full-color comic pages, where I got lost in the antics of *Broom-Hilda*, *Tiger*, *Beetle Bailey*, and *Boner's Ark*. Sometimes, my dad would pick up a dozen donuts on the way home; life was sweet and complete with a chocolate crème donut dropping powdered sugar onto the pages of my beloved comics.

As I got older, my interest expanded to include piles of *Peanuts* paperbacks, collected from yard sales and used book stores. Cheese puffs and cherry Kool-Aid replaced donuts as the snack of choice while poring over *Archie* comic digests, *Dennis the Menace,* and *Richie Rich.* These were the sacraments around which my Sunday-after-church ritual often revolved. (Ironically, cheese puffs are expressly banned during my comics workshops, for obvious, orange reasons.)

As an adult, I continue to be fascinated with comics and animated cartoons. A few years ago I was looking for a hook to use with young people who function within an increasingly image-saturated culture. An old *Peanuts* strip neatly articulates my struggle. In the first panel, Lucy is skipping rope when Linus approaches, blanket in hand. "Do you ever pray, Lucy?" he asks. Lucy replies, "That's kind of a personal question, isn't it? Are you trying to start an argument?" She becomes increasingly agitated: "I suppose you think you're somebody pretty smart, don't you?" she says in boldface. In the last panel, a shell-shocked Linus reports to Charlie Brown. "You're right . . . religion is a very touchy subject."[35]

Prayer is a particularly touchy subject. But does it have to be? Author and artist Sybil MacBeth wonders if prayer needs to be "a totally intense and serious activity. Can a spiritual practice be both prayer and play?"[36] I believe it can. My experience with youth groups has led me to embrace the power of humor to inform the act of praying and to radically change how one goes about teaching people about prayer. Prayer is, indeed, serious. But if prayer is authentic, it is also quirky, because we are quirky. It is through the quirky lens of pop-culturally-informed narrative that I approach the practice of prayer with my students.

A Case Study in Humor and Prayer

When the disciples ask Jesus to teach them to pray, we hear for the first time what will come to be known as the Lord's Prayer, and we learn a bit about what sort of outcomes we might expect when we pray. But it is on that first statement and how Jesus responds to it that guides this lesson on the outrageous nature of prayer.

The prayer Jesus teaches to his disciples is filled with words that are rich and evocative. Noun: Father. Adjective: Hallowed. Verb: Come. Adverb: Daily. It is like a holy game of Mad Libs.

Mad Libs is promoted as a "game for people who don't like games." As a youth minister, I have adopted Mad Libs as a useful teaching tool—a way to talk about prayer for people who don't like praying.

This is a word game that can be played alone or by any number of players. The instructions are described as "ridiculously simple." Each pad contains a series of stories with key words left out. One player selects a story. This player doesn't tell the other players what the story is about. Instead, she asks them for a series of words. These words—nouns, verbs, adjectives, and adverbs—are used to fill in the blank spaces. According to the creators of Mad Libs, when the completed page is read to the other players, they will discover that they have written a story that is "fantastic, screamingly funny, shocking, silly, crazy, or just plain dumb."

These may not be words that we ordinarily associate with prayer. When was the last time your prayers were screamingly funny? But why is that? What is it about prayer that makes us take it so seriously? According to Julia Cameron, we needn't be so uptight: "Prayer is talking to God. We can talk in a whisper. We can talk in a shout. We can talk in body language. We can talk in pictures. We can talk through music. We can talk through rhyme. What matters is less how we talk than that we talk."[37]

We can also talk through cartoons and comics. Teenagers often find that the language of traditional prayer is inaccessible, cumbersome, and downright confusing. It doesn't characterize the language of their everyday bumbling prayers. Perhaps this is why in my experience of working with kids, I see time and time again a reluctance to pray. Because they can't keep up with the traditional language, they think their prayers are going to sound "just plain dumb." This is patently untrue. I once asked for a volunteer to close out a youth group meeting with a prayer. After a period of awkward silence during which no one would make eye contact with me, one young man bravely agreed to try. We stood in a circle, bowed our heads, and closed our eyes. "God," he said, "You're great. Amen." A chorus of "Amens" and some giggling ensued, but I was struck by the simplicity and profound truth in those four words. Like the Mad Libs instructions suggest about the word game, prayer too can be "ridiculously simple."

I shared this story during the St. John's youth group meeting when we first began exploring the language of prayer. There were the expected groans when I introduced the topic, which turned into cautious interest when I insisted that prayer didn't have to be hard or boring but could, in fact, be fun. We started with the prayer book. After reading aloud the collect of the day, which included such phrases as "penitent hearts," "steadfast faith," and "unchangeable truth," I posed the question, "OK, so what did that just say?" Unsurprisingly, I was greeted by a series of blank stares and mumbling.

These teens are not the first ones to have trouble with the language of prayer. We might imagine a similar response of mumbles and blank looks from the disciples. After all, it is they who ask Jesus, "Lord, teach us to pray." We hear over and over that the disciples miss the point of sermons and parables, and Jesus is forever taking them aside to explain to them in simpler more mundane terms what he has just said. And what Jesus gives them is not so much a formula as a way to structure the vocabulary they already have. He fills in the blanks and he fills them in using words he knows will resonate with the disciples and make sense to them.

One year, the youth group took on the task of filling in the blanks, Mad Libs style. Through a series of exercises, we discovered our prayers as much as we wrote them. We learned that prayer can stretch the way we use our vocabulary and be ridiculously simple at the same time. Here is an example of a prayer written in less than five minutes by one of our youth group members:

God of all creation, you made the pale yellow walls of my
bedroom and the ebony black of my neighbor's saxophone.
Open our eyes to see you everywhere, in everything.

In everything. We discovered that prayer could be silly as we included robots, polar bears, and bunnies in our intercessions.

We also learned that, like playing a game of Mad Libs, the act of prayer could be undertaken alone or by any number of people together.

Our meeting came full circle as we shifted from individual prayers to the now-slightly-less-daunting task of writing our own collect:

> Gracious God, you are spectacular! We ask you to help us be happier and to heal the planet and everyone on it. Help us to make better choices; help us to help others. We ask this through Jesus Christ, who protects us from evil and does some pretty cool stuff.

This prayer is neither "screamingly funny" nor "just plain dumb." It is an honest prayer put together by considering a series of questions: What is God like? What do you want to ask of God? How can you make the world a better place? These young people followed Jesus's lead in filling in the blanks; but they did so using a combination of straightforward language, thoughtful consideration of what's relevant to them, youthful enthusiasm, and a little bit of humor.

It was ridiculously simple.

Although I do teach kids about prayer and its many varieties and functions, I would never presume to teach anyone *how* to pray. I would, however, encourage those who struggle with prayer—and I am one of them—to find a balance between the lofty, poetic language of tradition and our own language of pale yellow walls, ebony black saxophones, and pretty cool stuff.

Big Words

Pairing the silly words of the Mad Lib with images is the next logical step. Robert Short notes that the word "parable" translates into "word-picture" and goes so far as to suggest that these lessons are like "cartoons of the Bible."[38] Short is not the only one to point out that while Jesus may not have been intentionally comical, he certainly made ample use of paradox, exaggerations, irony, absurdity, and what Elton Trueblood terms "deliberately preposterous statements" in order to make his point known.[39]

A study of religion in the funny pages posits that "religion and humor share certain functional affinities."[40] Many cartoonists have enjoyed success poking fun at prayer and organized religion, at times blurring the line between offensive commentary and playful irreverence. For the purposes of curricular inclusion, I focus here on comics and cartoons that can be said to treat prayer as it often exists–sincere, challenging, and, if we are honest, a bit absurd. Comic strips and books are more likely to allude to religious practice as a whole than to specifically tackle prayer, but there are a few that dare to address this "touchy subject." Hank Ketchum's *Dennis the Menace* and Bil Keane's *Family Circus* characters are classic examples of kids who demonstrate both naïveté and profundity in their prayer lives. In one such strip, Dennis is seen kneeling at his bedside, hands folded, eyes closed. "Sorry," he says, "I don't know all those big words like our preacher does."[41]

While researchers Lindsey and Hereen argue that the children portrayed in the comics demonstrate a "lack of appreciation of the seriousness of religious matters,"[42] I propose that the opposite is true: These fictional children's honesty and curiosity can reveal the true nature of prayer. Similarly, it is my contention that the children and youth in our church programs approach prayer with an open-mindedness and simplicity from which we as educators, ministers, and persons of faith can learn. If cartoons and comics are places where people "grapple with issues of ethics, meaning, and values; engage in ritualized behavior; and explore both traditional and new"[43] religious practices, then it follows that this medium consisting of words and pictures can both inform and enrich the religious narrative.

The young people we encounter in church school and youth groups are indeed grappling. In my experience, humor not only softens their unwillingness to pray but also offers them permission to be themselves in the process. They don't necessarily *need* the "big words" that the preacher uses in order to pray authentically.

Trueblood asserts that the "widespread failure to recognize and appreciate the humor of Christ is one of the most amazing aspects of the era named for Him . . . [r]eligion, we think, is serious business, and serious business is incompatible with banter."[44] Contemporary cartoonists like David Wilkie and Cuyler Black, who often connect prayer with humor, know that it is within the banter that truth often reveals itself.

Wilkie accomplishes the task of connecting prayer and humor in his unusual strip, *Coffee with Jesus*. His characters, replete with foibles, doubts, and misplaced priorities, seek to draw closer to God through conversation . . . that is to say, through prayer. Wilkie admits that one of his goals is to introduce readers to "a practical savior, one who use(s) humor, sarcasm and gentle ribbing to address their concerns."[45] Here is a conversation between Carl and Jesus:

> *Carl*: Back then, in Bible times, did you have a sense of humor, Jesus?
> *Jesus*: Nope. Walked around dead serious, somber. Once in a while I could muster a weak smile when kids came up to me. Or puppies.
> *Carl*: Bummer. I'd always thought you were fully human as well as being fully God . . . Wait. You're playing with me, aren't you, J-Man?
> *Jesus*: Gotcha! So, a Catholic and a Baptist walk into a bar . . . stop me if you've heard this one.[46]

For years, strips like Johnny Hart's *B.C.* has been a frequent source of religious commentary. Hart himself considers his strip to be a ministry, "using it as a pulpit to communicate his Christian message."[47] Today, cartoonist Cuyler Black addresses the place of humor in ministry in an interview found on his *Inherit the Mirth* website. His response to a question about the balance between humor and offense:

> I like to think of my humor as being playfully reverent, or reverently playful. I love God. I'm excited to help emphasize an often under-appreciated facet of His personality—His humor. I always pray that He'll keep me within boundaries acceptable to Him. When it comes to having some fun with folks like Moses or Noah or the disciples, for example, I see them as fair game for some affectionate laughs at their expense because they're human like you and me, with flaws and foibles. When it comes to Jesus, I'll use Him in my cartoons but never make fun of Him. The humor will lie somewhere other than at His expense. And speaking of Jesus, I believe that much of His ministry involved a core message of "Hey, people, lighten up!"[48]

How *do* we lighten up? If, as theologian Karl Barth maintains, "Laughter is the closest thing to God's grace,"[49] it stands to reason that developing a theology of prayer that involves humor is not just desirable, but imperative.

Newspaper comics that do refer to or include prayer tend to focus on topics that are in some way universal. We laugh when *Nancy* prays for a freak snowstorm in May, because we know that we have prayed for ridiculous things for ridiculous reasons. We laugh when *Get Fuzzy*'s Bucky Katt worships the electric can opener, because we, too, have been guilty of misplaced loyalties, praise, and adoration. We laugh when Jon's bedtime prayers are interrupted by the sound of Garfield opening the refrigerator, because we know how difficult it can be to pray in the midst of hectic lives and competing demands for our attention, however noble our intentions may be.

We laugh because religion is a touchy subject. We laugh because religion is really about relationship and relationships can be, if we are at all honest, screamingly funny. Let us laugh.

CHAPTER 4

Super Faith

Archetypal Heroes and Religious Themes

He was a man like the rest of us.

*He had never seen himself as a champion, never considered himself
someone who might fearlessly face and fight the forces of evil.
But that, of course, was before he became . . . A SUPERHERO!*

—Stan Lee[50]

What makes a hero? The protagonist in Marvel's 1984 *Generic Comic Book* exemplifies the typical comic book conventions of super-heroism. This tongue-in-cheek issue follows the exploits of an unnamed man who, having been ineffective against a group of muggers, angrily smashes a souvenir snow globe that happens to contain some sort of radioactive substance. Upon awakening and discovering that he has a variety of powers, the fellow decides he needs a superhero suit to complement his newfound gifts. Naturally, he visits the Superhero Suit Store, where he purchases the most inexpensive, basic suit—a white, nondescript uniform complete with matching boots, mask, and cape. His subsequent adventures are more or less formulaic—which, of course, is the entire point of the generic comic.

Asking students about the nature of heroism is a great entry point into the study of prayer, scripture, and service. Most will immediately identify the traditional characteristics of superheroes with a list of superficial attributes: extra-human strength, archenemy, secret lair, cape. An examination of what each of these attributes represents can be helpful. Can one simply acquire the trappings of a hero? Opening the topic for debate by introducing Edna Mode of *The Incredibles* and her admonition, "No capes!" is an easy way to get kids to move past those symbols of heroism to the nature of heroic behavior itself.

Heroic characters, whether fictional, religious, or historical, tend to follow a similar trajectory. Anthropologist Joseph Campbell unwittingly assessed the generic comic book structure when he observed the recurring structuring of the archetypal hero's journey. Greg Garrett summarizes Campbell's conception of the hero's journey neatly:

> The basic shape of the archetypal hero's story is simple. It begins with the character in the *ordinary world,* everyday life. The character is then presented with some challenge, a *call to adventure,* a call that is sometimes refused. After finally accepting that call to heroism, the character must cross a *threshold* between the ordinary world and the world of adventure, after which, through trials, adventures, and the intervention of enemies and allies, he or she must muster courage to approach the inner sanctum of the enemy and undergo an *ordeal* that leads to a boon or reward of some sort. The hero then brings the reward back to society, but not without first facing an ultimate test of worth, which sometimes brings figurative or even literal death to the character before a sort of *resurrection* occurs.[51]

Garrett goes on to examine the parallels between mainstream comic heroes and biblical themes and characters. The most obvious and noteworthy of these comparisons is between Jesus and Superman. Much has been written about the similarities and messianic themes in the Superman canon; indeed, an exposition of the religious undertones of Superman could be and has been the subject of entire books. Suffice it to say here that there are compelling arguments for Superman as a Jesus figure, beginning with Superman's given name, Kal-El, which in Hebrew translates to "All that is God." Any number of biblical stories can serve as examples of Campbell's archetypal model.

From Superman and the Fantastic Four to the prophets and apostles, the stories follow the same basic pattern he identifies. Unpacking the hero's journey can be a useful exercise in your youth program or Bible study, especially when it is used within the context of sanctifying the ordinary acts of heroism of which we are all capable. It also provides a series of useful writing prompts and opportunities to develop character or plot:

- Choose a story from the Old or New Testament. Create a game board (think *Candyland*) or map of the hero's journey in comic form.

• Select a biblical hero. Explore and illustrate one aspect of the hero's journey.

• Pick a parable and create an alternate ending.

• Identify a hero from Scripture and tell the story from the villain's point of view.

• Go deeper. Illustrate what you would do if you were called to step in as the hero.

• Compare a Bible story to a comic book story. Then compare these to the story of someone who has been a hero to you in your own life.

• Compare and contrast the journeys of religious figures from different faith traditions. Make a comic timeline of events in the lives of each.

What does the hero's journey have to do with prayer and worship? As soon as we enter into relationship with God, which I define as prayer, we are taking our foot off of the firm foundation of the everyday and stepping over Campbell's threshold into the realm of the divine. Within this "region of supernatural wonder," we encounter God and are transported to a place of simultaneous vulnerability and power. We cycle through the hero's journey again and again with each bold prayer.

Furthermore, the very shape of our Anglican liturgy conforms, in its own way, to Campbell's conception of the archetypal hero's story. In the first place, the celebration of the Holy Eucharist places us squarely in the midst of Jesus's hero journey and creates in us active participants. Consider once again Campbell's story arc: "A hero ventures forth from the world of common day into a region of supernatural wonder: fabulous forces are there encountered and a decisive victory is won: the hero comes back from this mysterious adventure with the power to bestow boons on his fellow man."[52] Compare this to John Westerhoff's breakdown of the liturgy: Gather in the Lord's name; proclaim and respond to the Word of God; pray for the world and for the church; exchange the peace; prepare the table; make Eucharist; break the bread; share the gifts of God; go forth to love and serve.[53]

Whether we are entering the act of personal devotion or communal worship, we are figuratively or literally moving from the ordinary world to that of supernatural wonder. The collects, lessons, and sermon invite us into this world of adventure in much the same way that the opening panels of a comic book invite us into the action. We cross the threshold when we state our beliefs in the words of the creed, after which we wrestle with the ordeal of suffering and sin through our recitation of prayers for allies and enemies. We encounter fabulous forces as we receive absolution and share God's peace with our neighbors. In the enactment of the Great Thanksgiving, we walk with Christ and emerge victorious through the resurrection. Perhaps most importantly, we are dismissed with the mandate to take this "boon" out into the world with us, using this power to help others in their journeys.

This breakdown provides a framework for further investigation, and is a great way to get your youth group to pay attention during the liturgy. Before they enter a service of Holy Eucharist, distribute pens and notebooks or paper on clipboards. Invite the kids to trace the hero's journey as it unfolds in the pages of your worship service bulletin. Through notes and drawings, identify where Campbell's model of the archetypal hero aligns with the order of worship, and where it doesn't. Who is the hero in the Gospel of the day, and how does he or she fit into the formula? At which points during the liturgy are you asked to act on someone else's behalf? What does it look like to have the strength and courage to love and serve God, to be faithful witnesses?

Another useful place for this kind of inquiry is within the context of confirmation preparation. The Baptismal Covenant is in essence a prayer about the continuation of the hero's journey. The Rite of Confirmation's baptismal renewal asks us, once again, to cross the threshold from ordinary to extraordinary, marching teenagers through a divine adventure. From resisting evil to striving for justice and peace, candidates for confirmation are charged to take radical steps that sound like they came directly out of the pages of something from Marvel or DC.

From ancient biblical scrolls to newsprint preserved in a cheap plastic sleeve, it is hard to resist the superhero story. Such stories open us to the possibilities for greatness in ourselves and in others. Reading and creating comic books enable young people to explore such stories—stories that are not always linear—in a format that is both visually appealing and conducive to abrupt plot twists and leaps of faith.

CHAPTER 5
Saints and Sidekicks
Cultivating the Outrageous

> Believe it or not, it's just me.

—theme from *The Greatest American Hero*[54]

One of the first slides I show during my workshops is a *Peanuts* comic strip from the early nineties. An uncharacteristically jubilant Charlie Brown dances and cartwheels up the front walk, announcing: "I hit a home run in the ninth inning, and we won! I was the hero!!" His sister, Sally, is incredulous. "You?!" she asks.[55]

"Yes, you!" the reader wants to shout. The unlikeliest, most outrageous candidate is capable of and called to the heroic enterprise. There is no shortage of outrageous characters in comic books. When you survey the comics and cartoon canon, you will find many such ridiculous characters, from the popular *Teenage Mutant Ninja Turtles* and the *Tick* to the more obscure, like *Too Much Coffee Man* and, one of my childhood favorites, *Sprocket Man*, a public service tale of a benevolent but vaguely menacing superhero who promotes bicycle safety and single-handedly thwarts the evil plans of would-be bike thieves.

The adventures of an unlikely superhero of my own creation are chronicled in *Tales from the Lint Trap*, a self-published mini-comic. In each issue, one can follow the exploits of Missing Sock Man, a seemingly ordinary sock that has become lost in the laundry. Every Tuesday, Missing Sock Man ventures out through the dryer vent in search of crimes to prevent and problems to solve. The premise behind Missing Sock Man

Heather J. Annis

is fundamentally absurd, but it is a lot of fun to write and makes me laugh. It also makes me think about the rather dull and boring subject of laundry in a fresh and even prayerful way. Drawing cartoons can be a study not only in humor, but also in the practice of mindfulness. Being aware of the holy in the midst of the mundane is one of the conditions that makes prayer possible.

Prayer can feel every bit as absurd as the exploits of a caped sock, which can be used to one's advantage in a teaching situation. Kids particularly appreciate the miracle of absurdity. If you have any doubt at all about the veracity of this statement, consider for a moment the popularity of a certain animated yellow sponge who lives in a pineapple under the sea and flips burgers for a living. Recall some of the superheroes of your childhood. Visit any independent publishing convention or comic book store and you will find hundreds of examples of ridiculous characters and scenarios. Comics and cartoons cater to our fascination with the outrageous—from masked superheroes and their bumbling sidekicks to the adventures in which they become entangled.

Not only is the comics industry rife with alarmingly silly characters, the potential for publishing such silliness is made clear by another slide I regularly show of a newspaper comic strip called *Monorail High*. This particular strip is about a piece of chewing gum that has been stuck under a desk. That's it. In the final panel of the strip, the piece of gum states, "I'm just gum."[56] That this googly-eyed, raisin-like glob of bubblegum made it onto newsprint and thus, into the comic lexicon, I offer as evidence that no character, no story, no individual is too ridiculous to have something to say.

Like the creators of these characters, God has a definite knack for choosing unlikely candidates for servitude and heroism. A poster on my office door wonders, "Do you seriously think God can't use you?" The question is followed by a list of twenty-five biblical personages who can only be described as ordinary, everyday people going about their lives and each has his or her own case against being heroic. "Abraham was too old," the poster proclaims. "Moses had a stuttering problem," "the disciples fell asleep," and startlingly, "Lazarus was dead." As we all know, this litany of ordinary people performs powerful acts and demonstrates extraordinary faith despite their faults, doubts, and altogether unexceptional day-to-day attributes.

Comics can be an effective way to engage young people in conversation about their own potential for heroism. Using the language of cartoon characters also makes discipleship relevant and authentic to a demographic of human beings whose potential is often dismissed or overlooked. Like Charlie Brown, famous for his ordinariness, we should recognize and rejoice at the opportunity to accomplish something marvelous.

It is patently absurd that Jesus should select for his disciples a motley assortment of fishermen, tax collectors, and general riffraff. This absurdity is what makes many comic book heroes so appealing and resonant with youth. According to Greg Garrett, what appeals to us about a character like Spiderman is that he is "just like us, an ordinary person."[57] That someone like Charlie Brown or something as mundane as an odd sock could have a contribution to make sends a message to the forgotten and disenfranchised. It is an empowering notion that has much to say about the ability of God to work his wonders through us.

Prayer and Silliness

In his book on arts ministry, Michael Bauer talks about "sanctifying the ordinary."[58] Prayer and the spiritual life are very much about seeing the mundane as important, even holy. A *Cul de Sac* strip by Richard Thompson shows young Petey being driven home from his first day of cartoon camp. He is telling his mother that the instructor wants his students to draw comics "about our everyday lives. He said it could be boring, dull, *and* uneventful!" Petey goes on to say that he is planning to create a fifteen-page comic about a "spot on my ceiling."[59] You can't get much more mundane than that.

So, what does this have to do with prayer? For starters, prayer is seldom an earth-shattering occurrence. Prayer happens in the midst of the everyday, and can be undertaken while kneeling in a pew in church, doing your math homework, or chopping carrots in your kitchen. Prayer is about elevating the most ordinary of concerns to an extraordinary level of attention.

That the disciples fall asleep while praying with Jesus tells us something we already know: Prayer is not necessarily an exciting endeavor. When I first hold up a Book of Common Prayer and ask my students to "Tell me what you know about this red book," two of the most common responses are that it is "long" and "boring." The poetry and ritual of the prayer book is often lost on young people who are accustomed to receiving and supplying information in short, abbreviated form. The language of the Book of Common Prayer, while beautiful, can be difficult for kids to access—it is as foreign to them as it would be if it were written in Klingon.

Robert Pazmiño suggests that "one major task in the ministries of Christian education is sharing the Christian story and enabling others to appropriate that story in relation to their lives."[60] It is often difficult for young people to believe that their prayers matter to God, that they themselves, in fact, matter to God. In many cases, prayer has become an endeavor reserved for those with the "right" words and the "right" intentions. Comics can mediate this tension between the mundane and the holy by introducing a sort of holy silliness, an understanding that prayer is available and accessible to anyone who cares to entertain the ridiculous idea that a spot on the ceiling or a piece of chewing gum could be worthy of attention; that *they* are worthy of attention. It is our job as ministers, educators, and comics nerds to enable kids to envision themselves as faithful witnesses and servants. It is a ridiculous notion, but it may also be the most important notion to believe and communicate to our congregations, church schools, and youth groups.

Celebrating silliness does not mean that we dismiss convention and common sense. It means that by sanctifying the ordinary, we make relevant that which might otherwise be overlooked. What could be more ordinary than a few loaves of bread and a couple of fish? Who could be a more unlikely savior than the son of a carpenter?

To embrace their own capacity for the heroic is to empower kids to assess their talents, strengths, and interests in a God-centered manner. Paradoxically, recognizing and valuing their ordinariness can instill in them a sense of humility and need for God's grace. My favorite comic strip illustration of this tension is a *Calvin and Hobbes* strip featuring Calvin as Stupendous Man: We encounter Calvin struggling to get into his "Stupendous Man" costume. Hands behind his back, Hobbes innocently asks, "Superheroes wear snowpants?"

"When there's snow out, they do!" an exasperated Calvin retorts.

In the last panel, Hobbes taunts Calvin, who complains, "Well, of course the zipper's going to get stuck if everyone stands around watching me!"[61]

Besides being just plain funny, this strip portrays in brilliant fashion the acute state of being simultaneously ordinary and extraordinary. We know from previous strips that Stupendous Man is capable of astonishing acts (admittedly not always heroic, but usually nefarious and self-serving), aided by a homemade costume and cape. As we watch Calvin struggling into his snowsuit, we ought to recognize our own struggles to fit into the people God calls us to be.

Whether our vision of being heroes involves saving the world as Stupendous Man or winning a baseball game like Charlie Brown, the bottom line is that we are called to be disciples. Believe it or not, it's just me. It's just you. It's just all of us muddling through our jobs and schoolwork and prayers and pleas.

And I Mean to Be One, Too

In the episode entitled, "The Father, the Son, and the Holy Guest Star," Bart Simpson is given a copy of the *Lives of the Saints* comic book. After reading it, he pronounces it to be much better than the other magazines and comic books in the dentist's waiting room.

Although the comic book industry has set a small but noteworthy precedent when it comes to saints and saint-like figures, I wish the comic book *Lives of the Saints* were a real thing. At any rate, the presence or absence of real-life saints in the comics presents a ripe opportunity for discussion and illustration with your group. The Roman Catholic Church pays a good deal of attention to saints; the current pontiff, Pope Francis—who is himself the subject of a comic book—shares this about aspiring to sainthood: "To be saints is not a privilege for the few . . . sanctity is a vocation for everyone."[62]

An entry by blogger Mike Hatrick describes his experience with a school project.[63] When he was ten years old, Mike decided to do his homework assignment on the life of St. Patrick, in comic book form. I was immediately interested in his story, but was disappointed to learn that his creative, non-conformist approach to his project was neither acknowledged nor celebrated. I often encounter stories like this in my workshops and I make it my mission to make sure it doesn't happen to kids in my groups. In honor of Mike's experience, I offer some ways to include this art form in your work in this area.

A handful of saints and holy figures have made their way into the comics canon, among them Francis of Assisi and Mother Teresa. Along with the apostles, many of these saints appear on holy cards. Traditionally, these devotionals are about the size of baseball cards and portray

Jesus or the saints in a soft, painterly manner. On the back there is usually a prayer attributed to or relevant to the person pictured. These somewhat old-fashioned mementos may seem stuffy to teenagers, but they make for the basis of a great lesson plan.

Prayers and Personal Heroes

A prayer card by Brother Mickey McGrath featuring a stylized drawing of Teresa of Avila, along with an inspirational quote, inspired the following exercise. The only supplies you will need are pencils and unlined index cards. (You can also use artist trading cards, which are made of heavier stock than index cards and are available at most art supply stores.) On one side of the card, ask students to write down the name of their favorite religious saint and to list any facts about this person. On the other side, identify a person whom they consider to be a saint in their own lives. Once these steps are completed, it is helpful to go a little deeper. What is it about the people they have chosen that makes them "saints"? What qualities do they have? What makes them different from other folks? Next, invite participants to create their own holy cards.

One member of our youth group wrote about his friend Paul, who is always there for him and is always kind. Another created a card in memory of a favorite cousin who had died at a young age. In the first case, Brian illustrated his holy card with a character his friend had created. Lock, on the other hand, was reticent about drawing a portrait (at least without a photograph as a reference) so instead chose to draw a jar of fireflies—a reminder of good times with Jessie. In this case, the exercise led to the creation of a new character, a giant firefly named Richard, whose sole mission is to guide those who are lost.

Here are a couple of related activities:

• Make comics in which your favorite historical saints meet your personal heroes. What happens? Do they do battle to determine who is more saintly? Do they band together to defeat some mutual foe?

• Write and illustrate your own verses to the tune of "I Sing a Song of the Saints of God." [64]

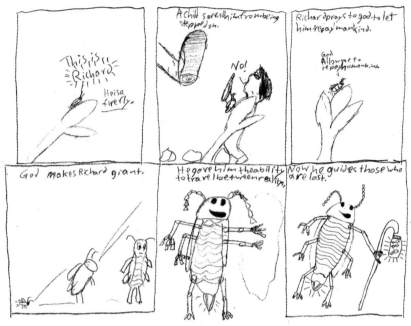

Lock Billingsley

Good and Faithful Servants

We all have the potential to be super; many aspire to be heroes in one way or another. The reality is that most of us end up as sidekicks. There is no shame in this. Batman needs Robin; Fred needs Barney; Jesus needs the disciples. At times, the sidekick is imbued with similar or complementary powers. Robin has become a hero in his own right, with a DC comic book series all his own. Barney is clearly the mental superior to Fred Flintstone, but his main characteristic is a fierce loyalty to his best friend. The disciples, who can be infuriatingly thick-headed, are given the abilities to heal, to cast out demons, to preach, and to evangelize.

In his second letter to Timothy, Paul says that, in addition to multiple gifts, we are given the spirit of power and love (2 Tim. 1:7). Our personal powers are powers which we are called to use for many purposes, some noble, others practical. All are to be used in service, as we act as God's sidekicks in the world. Explore the attributes of sidekicks using the following exercises.

Matching Game

The Bible is filled with stories of heroes and sidekicks. I always cite the disciples as Jesus's sidekicks, because they are the type of sidekicks that we often are—loyal, but a little confused as to our roles and largely clueless about the gifts and powers God has given us. But there are other tales of sidekicks who truly fulfill their duties to the heroes they accompany and serve. For this activity, students will need to match the sidekick to his or her hero. Here are some examples of biblical pairings:

Lot/Abraham	Ruth/Naomi
Joshua/Moses	Jonathan/David
Barak/Deborah	Barnabas/Paul
Samuel/Eli	

You can also include a bunch of duos from popular culture:

Piglet/Winnie-the-Pooh	Robin/Batman
Patrick/Spongebob	Rocket J. Squirrel/Bullwinkle
Spock/Captain Kirk	Watson/Sherlock Holmes

List sidekicks in one column and heroes in another and have kids draw a line to connect the pairs to each other. Have a prize ready for the person who gets the most correct answers. Ask the group to identify other pairs that are not on the list. Use this opportunity to talk about the heroes and sidekicks in their everyday lives.

Dynamic Duos

Divide your class into two groups of equal size; have them meet in separate rooms if possible. Have each member of one group invent superheroes. Each hero should have a name, a super-power, and a mission. Try to be more specific than "to save the world." Save the world from what? An evil villain? Acid rain? Killer donuts? In the other room, have the group members create sidekicks. Each sidekick should have a name, a weakness or flaw, and a ridiculous talent. Have each kid write the word "Hero" or "Sidekick" on one side of an index card, and write their characters' three attributes on the reverse.

After a predetermined amount of time, bring your groups back together into a common meeting space. Randomly assign each person from the hero group a sidekick partner. Each pair must then come up with a story and illustrations using the qualities of both characters to approach and solve the mission identified on the hero card.

A variation on this theme is to have everyone in the group design sidekicks based on their own real or imagined qualities; pair each sidekick with God or Jesus and a predetermined mission (such as to feed the hungry, build the Church, heal the sick, and so on).

CHAPTER 6

"Mr. Peace" Be with You

A Case Study in Community Art-Making

"What is the use of a book," thought Alice, "without pictures or conversations?"

—Lewis Carroll[65]

It all started with a piece of white muslin and a purple fabric marker. Members of the St. John's youth group were making prayer flags for our children's chapel. Subjects ranged from flowers and rainbows to intricate designs and smiley faces. One flag stood out. On it was depicted a shady-looking fellow with purple stubble and a long, twirling handlebar mustache. Both arms were raised, hands flashing crude peace signs. Its creator, a mischievous red-headed sixth-grader named Ben, laughingly held up his flag and told us that the round-faced man's name was "Mr. Peace." Not expecting to be taken seriously, Ben was surprised when I demanded that he label his flag and announced that we might just have been introduced to the main character of our comic book project.

The next few weeks of youth group get-togethers centered on conversations about superheroes, discipleship, the nature of God, and qualities of sidekicks. We filled page after page of flipchart paper responding to such questions as, "What are the qualities of superheroes? How do these qualities overlap with the qualities of God? What does it mean to be a disciple or sidekick? How can you develop your own God-given superpowers to benefit others?"

The result of this speculation is a ludicrous story featuring the strange adventures of a character called Mr. Peace.

By day, Mr. Peace operates a factory that manufactures fake mustaches. The factory employs a cadre of smiling pigs . . . and one goat.

Ben Geoghegan

Mr. Peace drives a VW bus, captains a starship, and has the power to heal and spread peace wherever he goes. Unable to speak, he communicates telepathically; sometimes he is understood, other times not—but he always understands the needs of the people and creatures he encounters. Like Jesus, Mr. Peace is dedicated to healing and the business of salvation. Like Jesus, Mr. Peace is not always easily recognizable, even by those closest to him. And like Jesus, Mr. Peace deputizes a rather motley crew of sidekicks to help spread his gospel of love and peace.

One of Mr. Peace's most ridiculous, and yet significant, features is his ability to prevent recognition by the application of a simple false moustache. Like many popular superheroes who wear masks and other costumes to keep their identities secret, Mr. Peace looks like an ordinary guy in his everyday life. Our hero wears a hooded sweatshirt (an ersatz trench coat) in which is concealed a variety of pockets containing false moustaches. In addition to serving as ready disguises that allow him to keep his true identity a secret, these fuzzy adhesive objects give Mr. Peace various powers, from stealth movement, to healing the sick, to preparing the perfect omelet.

Conversations

As silly as Mr. Peace can be, he is unmistakably a Jesus figure. The most compelling question Mr. Peace caused our youth group to ask was "Why do we have so much trouble recognizing the savior in our midst and the disciples in ourselves?" They explored these questions in a sermon, demonstrating the depth of conversation elicited by a simple cartoon.

Mr. Peace's ability to enlist the most ordinary and unlikely personages (including pigs and goats) to help him accomplish his mission of peace is a profound and radical message. Instead of having one bumbling sidekick, Mr. Peace simply latches onto the handiest bystander and slaps a false moustache on his or her face. In this way, the everyday is transformed into the "super" as we are pressed into service in unexpected circumstances.

The obvious absurdity of Mr. Peace parallels the outrageous idea that God calls on us to do his work in the world. He calls us to peace and healing and to embrace our inherent heroic qualities even in our human imperfection.

So, how did we get from a humble sketch on a piece of cloth to this kind of theological discourse? One way was to be intentional about asking questions about the nature of heroes, sidekicks, and living lives of faith.

Getting Started

How you begin your conversation is partially dependent on the size of your group. The larger the group, the more winnowing steps you will have to build in to ensure that you both honor everyone's ideas and put these ideas together in such a way as to make sense. One way to begin is to have a predetermined theme generated by leaders. Brainstorm a list of potential topics such as peace, prayer, discipleship, miracles, healing, parables, and so forth. A clear theme generally emerges that seems naturally to fit the size, maturity level, and interests of your youth group or church school.

Once you have the theme, remember that while this theme will guide each set of meetings and activities, I recommend that you keep track

Heather Annis

of ideas that seem to deviate from it. Often such ideas provide a helpful counterpoint to the story that you will develop. For example, if you decide to create a superhero whose focus is on healing, the existence of diseases that remain incurable may lead you to a perfect villain.

Keep current events in mind. In this example, topics in the recent news such as the Ebola virus and measles outbreaks have the potential to generate meaningful conversation about why sickness exists and what God's role in it is. Remain open to suggestions that might seem "anti-God" and put those suggestions into play in the actions of your hero's opponent. Opposing views on the Bible, current events, power, and responsibility provide grist for the creative mill and should not be dismissed unless they are hurtful or offensive.

Spend lots of time making lists. Learning to brainstorm effectively without judgment is a critical skill that kids will use long after your comic project is complete. Allow the suggestions to be ludicrous, while relating each to the theme whenever possible.

Art Trauma and Not Messing Up

No matter the size or age of your group, it is imperative to address something I call "art trauma." More pervasive in groups of adults, this phenomenon seems to stem from experiences in which someone has been told his or her artwork is not "correct." While producing artwork that is appealing and satisfying is certainly a goal, creating an environment for art-making that is safe, productive, meaningful, and fun is far more important.

Cartoonist and writer Lynda Barry describes the art trauma phenomenon in her comic *Two Questions*. She talks about a time when drawing was freeing and alive, before the creative process was hijacked by the questions, "Is this good? Does this suck?" These questions plague artists and non-artists alike; neither is constructive, but you will encounter both in your comic-making work. Drawing can be intimidating, especially in a group setting. Nevertheless, Barry implores us: "To all the kids who quit drawing, come back!"[66]

It is this invitation to "come back" that drives my work making art of all kinds with people of all kinds. Getting your young people to come back to that place of playful creation is vital to the comic book enterprise and can be applied to any number of religious situations you may be covering in your curriculum. From prayer to drawing cartoons to how they look in acolyte robes, silliness and acceptance are equal partners in making art together in the teenaged faith community.

Once we had our theme and had invited our kids to "come back," we broke our large group into smaller teams of four or five, each with a specific theme on which to work: developing the mustache story-line, designing Mr. Peace's various modes of transportation, identifying and creating an arch-enemy in the sinister Carl Crump and his inept brother, Barry, and so on. Each team was responsible for listing each character's attributes, potential plot twists, and "props" that Mr. Peace would encounter throughout his adventure. These small groups would eventually translate into action, as we transformed the world of our comic book into a physical one for a spring fundraiser (see "The Cardboard Challenge" on page 48).

Art Is a Team Sport

Eventually it became clear that we needed to form an art team. I recommend this especially if you have more than fifteen or twenty kids in your program. Kids tend to self-select, although issuing personal invitations can encourage the reluctant child to consider the idea. There is no magic number of members; six to eight works well in terms of staying on task and giving individual attention. Such a team is a relatively low-maintenance group to run, requiring simple but good-quality materials, including basic art supplies: mechanical pencils, white erasers, rulers, black pens with medium and fine points, non-photo blue pencils, drawing and tracing paper, and, in St. John's case, spoons . . . for chocolate pudding. Most meetings begin with a drawing warm-up or writing exercise and an agenda listing a small number of priority tasks from which members are allowed to choose.

Our comic book art team continues to meet and has emerged as a group that embodies the creative dimension of youth group. With Abby having graduated and moved on to art school, the art team invited several new young members and is charged with the ongoing task of filtering the brainstorms of our youth group into manageable, marketable, and cohesive combinations of words and images. Art teams function as sort of an internal "spell check" for the ideas of the larger group. They also foster leadership skills, as members are challenged with selecting what materials to include and how, coming to consensus as a small group, and communicating their decisions to the larger group.

Art by committee can be a challenge, as seen when *Calvin and Hobbes* collaborate on a poster contest entry. Calvin comes up with the idea while Hobbes does all the drawing. They argue about how they will split the prize money—naturally, Calvin believes he deserves a bigger cut—until they angrily agree to divide the reward 50-50. Calvin stalks off with his poster, grumbling that, "A good compromise leaves everybody mad."[67]

The real trick is to build trust by including elements of every child's suggestion, no matter how silly or small, without letting any one member monopolize the creative process. This takes time, patience, and practice. In my workshops, I condense this year-long process into a matter of hours or a few days. What follows are some tips for starting the conversation regardless of how much time you have to devote to creating comics in your church school or youth group.

Practical Advice

Structuring Meetings

Open meetings with prayers from various sources, especially prayers written by group members. Include drawing warm-ups and/or writing prompts whenever possible. Examples are included in Appendix A. It is also easy to adapt a variety of ordinary games such as Pictionary, Uno, and Jenga for use as drawing and storytelling exercises.

Cultivate the outrageous. At this point, no idea is too ridiculous to consider. Write everything down without judgment. The rest will take care of itself as long as you and your young people remain open to the ludicrous possibilities God will offer.

Meet regularly for a predetermined period of time with a clear but flexible agenda. What are your goals and expectations for each gathering? Build in time for brainstorming and for tangents. Often the seemingly unrelated remark or doodle can become the basis for something extraordinary.

Understanding Heroes and Creating Characters

Study superheroes in popular culture. Bring in a selection of comic books, graphic novels, and zines—your local comic shop can help you with this. This is also a great time to show old episodes of the *Superfriends* or a movie like *The Incredibles*. Study superheroes in the Bible. Who are the most ludicrous heroes? Why did God choose them? How are they like (or unlike) the characters in comic books? What would you do if you were thrown into a biblical situation like the Great Flood or the Feeding of the Five Thousand? Who are the heroes in those stories?

Study heroes of the everyday. What have your students done that is heroic? Who are their real-life heroes and why? Identify the following characteristics of the hero you are creating: name, superpower, costume, secret identity, origin, sidekick, weakness, archenemy, favorite food, transportation, hangout, and signature slogan are great places to start. Often, kids like to apply these characteristics to the creatures they invent in the Exquisite Corpse exercise described in Appendix A. Occasionally, someone will prefer to create a supervillain instead of a hero. Let them!

Naming Your Characters

Naming is one of the most important aspects of comic character creation. A catchy name draws in potential readers and makes defining a character's identity less difficult. Long before Voldemort, there was "the Unnameable"—an "evil force so deadly that to know his name is to fall prey to his will."[68] Choosing a name for your characters sets the tone for the story and for the elements within it.

Using a name generator can be helpful in coming up with characters or story titles. I am partial to one I found online called "What's Your Anime Series Title?"[69] It assigns a descriptor to each letter in a person or place's name; for example, the name for St. John's Youth Group would be "Bubblegum Sushi Alchemy Overture." Play around with the words until you come up with something that seems irresistible.

Plot Development

Choosing the story you want to tell is important. Use a list of writing prompts and games to get started. See Appendix B for examples or generate your own. Rory's Story Cubes or a box of Story Cards can be invaluable to jumpstarting plots. Develop a storyline that is manageable, with a clear beginning, middle, and end. Storyboards are helpful; you can find a template online or easily create your own for this purpose. An abridged form of Joseph Campbell's archetypal hero's journey (see chapter 4) can help to guide plot development.

Production and Promotion

Start drawing! One or two students will likely emerge as your main illustrators. If you are envisioning a collaborative effort to create a single product, another cluster of kids can work on writing the story. Small groups work best here. Alternatively, individuals can create their own stand-alone mini-comics by using templates easily found online.[70]

Depending on your budget, you will have to determine whether you will reproduce your comic strip or book in black and white, color, or grayscale. For your first project, I recommend printing the pages in black and white. You can do this on any decent copier or printer using twenty-four-pound bright white paper. We did our cover in full color and had it printed on semi-gloss stock.

Market your product. Is your comic book something you will share outside of your class or youth group? Who is the audience for your book of mini-comics? We spoke about our Mr. Peace comic in a youth sermon, described the process in our church newsletter, and sold copies to raise funds for a youth mission trip. Determine a price point based on your fundraising goal and the perceived financial resources of your congregation.

As a surprise, I designed business cards for our youth group members. They were delighted to receive them and distributed them with the comic books they sold, showed them off at school, and proudly handed them to friends and relatives. The cards were an inexpensive and professional way to acknowledge the hard work and enthusiasm of the group.

Have fun! Set reasonable goals and expectations, but enjoy the process. The less you stress about deadlines, the richer an experience your kids will have.

The Cardboard Challenge

Our spring fundraiser was an unanticipated byproduct of our decision to sell *The Strange Adventures of Mr. Peace* to raise money for a youth mission trip. It was inspired by a viral YouTube video about nine-year-old Caine Monroy, who constructed a cardboard arcade in his father's auto parts shop and became an Internet sensation.[71] The St. John's inaugural "Cardboard Challenge" sought to bring elements of Mr. Peace's comic book world to life and served not only to entertain but also to invite parishioners into a three-dimensional version of Mr. Peace's otherwise flat world.

In the space of a few months, our church school wing was transformed into a sort of up-cycled theme park. The control room of Mr. Peace's starship, the USS Peacekeeper, was the site of a series of homemade carnival games from skee-ball to a mustache-themed bean-bag toss. Young children were able to swing a Wiffle ball bat at an enemy spacecraft piñata, have their pictures taken as caped superheroes "flying" over a cardboard city skyline, play pin the 'stache on Mr. Peace, and "drive" around in a brown VW bus with a suspender-like method of wearing the vehicle. Visitors wrote messages of peace on a rocket made from a giant tube used to store carpeting.

The Cardboard Challenge was an exercise in creativity and thrift. Youth group members lugged in cardboard boxes of all sizes and saved toilet paper tubes and egg cartons. We visited the local recycling center, where we purchased assorted tubes, cones, and other useful items for forty cents a pound. Kids made blueprints and drawings and demonstrated a level of effort and ingenuity that was rivaled only by the unusual quality of the world they created. As an extension of the comic book project, the fundraiser was both complement and supplement. The Cardboard Challenge enabled us to host an intergenerational event that raised a significant amount of money while at the same time offering a sneak peek into the ways in which our young people had been exploring the nature of discipleship.

While the youth group concentrated on the Cardboard Challenge, an even more focused team of four youth group members emerged as the story arc of the comic book became more developed and clear and the characters began to take shape. The art team's objective–in addition to eating chocolate pudding at every meeting (hence the reference to spoons earlier)—was to take all the ideas and sketches created by the larger group and turn them into a story and artwork that would hang together. We worked for several months converting crude drafts of Volkswagen vans, pigs wearing construction helmets, and complex schematics for spaceships and secret mustache formulas into consistently-drawn images with a comprehensible plot complete with cliffhanger.

Abby chose to contribute her incredible drawing skills to the comic book as part of her high school senior project. Once the art team had submitted storyboards and rough drafts of drawings, Abby translated them into a combination of brilliant manga-inspired pages. We spent hours uploading her drawings into Manga Studio[72] and Photoshop,[73] where she added background textures like starbursts and tiny dots and we inserted the textual elements: narrative, dialogue, and sound effects. After two weeks of scanning, inking, editing, and eating pad thai straight from the carton, we were ready for production.

The interior black and white pages were reproduced on our office copy machine; we had the covers printed in color on semi-gloss paper. The kids folded and stapled numerous copies, which were then sold as part of the spring fundraiser. Pierce happily strode around during coffee hours wearing a cardboard sandwich board, peddling comic books with great enthusiasm and success. The comic books sold out almost immediately, and we began work on the second issue, which was sold the following fall.

Going Forth

In the meantime, we invited our congregation to become active participants, not in the comic book per se, but in the overarching story. We created a paper version of Mr. Peace and provided opportunities for children and adults to color their own copy, each of which was then laminated. Mr. Fred Peace became Flat Freddy, who has his roots in *Flat Stanley*, a children's book by Jeff Brown, which has similarly inspired Flat Andy of the Episcopal Diocese of Texas, and many versions of Flat Jesus.

Church school kids brainstormed where they could take Flat Freddy. The playground, the circus, and the beach were popular suggestions.

Abigail Ray

Every Flat Freddy cutout was accompanied by an explanation and instructions:

> Jesus said, "Peace I leave with you; my peace I give you." Every Sunday we exchange the peace, saying, "Peace be with you." Flat Freddy is a tangible symbol of these messages; he is designed to be carried with you wherever you go as a reminder of God's peace and our responsibility to share that peace with those we meet.

Parishioners were invited to "Go forth *with* peace" and to take pictures of Flat Freddy wherever they went.

Heather Annis

By the end of that summer we posted photographs of Flat Freddy on his many adventures. There was Mr. Peace at Gillette Stadium, home of the New England Patriots. There were pictures of him posing with Smokey the Bear in New Hampshire, a pink dinosaur in Maine, and enjoying the seashore on Cape Cod. In addition to every New England state, Flat Freddy Peace was spotted in Florida, Nevada, North Carolina, New York, and Spain. He's gone camping, hiking, and to coffee shops. Photographing an expression of peace is not only fun, it is a method of cultivating mindfulness. It is also a form of visual prayer that can be shared with relative ease and with little to no discomfort.

The pictures and conversations generated by the making of comics give us profound glimpses of the holy. The images and stories behind Mr. Peace and other characters created in workshops (like the unlikely hero named Judas who battles Pharisees-turned-werewolves) provide what Will Eisner called "graphic witness,"[74] making visible the role of faith in the everyday life of young people.

CHAPTER 7

From Common to Comic

A Practical Approach

> The comics creator asks us to join in a silent dance of the seen and the unseen. The visible and the invisible.
>
> —Scott McCloud[75]

While the characters in comic books and graphic novels "might not always speak outwardly about religion and the Gospel, their storylines make implicit, and sometimes explicit, points about theology."[76] If one of the Church's tasks is to engage with culture,[77] then it must also, at times, seek to situate theological conversation within the context of popular culture. With the graphic novel being one of the fastest growing literary media in America,[78] it stands to reason that using the illustrative art form offers a unique opportunity to address prayer from a point of view that resonates with today's youth.

A simple search on the Internet immediately identifies 108 newspaper strips dealing with the subject of prayer. Beetle Bailey prays. Hagar the Horrible prays. Dennis the Menace and the members of *Family Circus* are often seen praying or engaged in other religious activities and conversations. Among others, characters from mainstream strips like *Pearls Before Swine, Mother Goose and Grimm, Opus, Bizarro,* and *Frank and Ernest* have also been depicted in prayer.

Each week our third- through fifth-grade class reads a story from Rob Suggs's *Comic Book Bible*. Then we ask two questions: "Who is the hero in this story?" "What would you do in this situation?" After some discussion and a related activity, we close our time together with this prayer from the Roots website, filling in the blank at the end with whomever the class has chosen as the hero of the day:

For the times when we have been less than heroic,
Lord we are sorry.
For the times we have not used our hero talents,
Lord we are sorry.
Give us the courage not to hide our potential
but to be generous,
not to dismiss others but to celebrate their gifts.
Encourage us to follow the example of

_____

and have a go at being heroes.
Amen.[79]

This is a practical example of what prayer can say about superheroes, but what do superheroes have to say about prayer? We encounter prayer in comic book form more often than one might guess. As a child, Bruce Wayne kneels beside his bed, hands folded. "Don't forget to say your prayers, Bruce," says Uncle Philip, closing the door behind him. Praying for the power to avenge his parents' deaths, young Bruce replies that he never forgets. "Please dear God—help me keep my promise! I'll do anything!" he cries.[80] Batman's mission to fight crime is born.

Prayer may not be the central topic of any mainstream comic book that I have come across, but that does not mean that prayer is absent from the medium. Religious themes and concerns pepper the pages of popular comic books; examples in which the topic is addressed directly can be found with well-known characters like *Daredevil*, *Spider-Man*, and the *X-Men*. There are also a few examples of using the comic book format to provide Christian prayer instruction, as in the case of Gene Luen Yang's *Comic Book Rosary* and *Dennis the Menace and the Bible Kids'* line-by-line treatment of the Lord's Prayer.

Despite the relative scarcity of prayer in comic book form (that it exists at all is noteworthy), the comic book can be a valuable tool for both prayer instruction and expression. Margaret Guenther suggests, "Surely the act of prayer is both infinitely simpler and infinitely more profound than we make it out to be."[81] With that in mind, I seek to design activities that are at once instructional and informative as well as fun, memorable, and relevant.

Talking openly about prayer can make people uncomfortable. Using newspaper strips and comics anthologies to jumpstart the conversation can be effective in groups and individual settings. Comics provide a forum in which to put prayer into common language using images and humor that are familiar and relevant. Through this medium, we can convey the urgency and disappointment of "unanswered" prayers as well as the intimacy and joy of a satisfying spiritual practice. Putting prayers on paper can be a daunting task for people of any age; working within the structure of comic book panels and word balloons gives the endeavor a manageable combination of levity and purpose.

Of the Book of Common Prayer, Guenther says that it is characterized by the word "common," meaning that the prayer book "belongs to all of us and is normally used when we come together, as well as being an excellent book of personal devotion. What we hold in common binds us together and cements the gloriously disparate pieces that make up our community."[82] If prayer belongs to all of us, this necessarily includes children and youth and their interpretations of prayers that are familiarly used in worship and individual practice. Using images to complement these prayers—as well as new iterations of these prayers—is the next logical step.

Prayer Made Visible

The idea of an illustrated prayer book is not a new one. Before the invention of the printing press, prayer books with hand-done lettering and illustrations were used to educate and enrich worship. The comic prayer books made by youth seek to combine this traditional pairing of text and images with elements of humor and creative interpretation of prayers done by young people.

In the current case, participants were predominantly middle school students. The program year began with an overview of different types and purposes of prayer: adoration, confession, thanksgiving, supplication, and intercession. Within these broad categories, we explored in depth certain portions of the Book of Common Prayer: collects, creeds, confessions, prayers of the people, the Psalms, canticles, and the Lord's Prayer. In addition, we discussed more generic types of prayer like table blessings and general thanksgivings. Throughout the course of the year, we did a variety of exercises designed to aid in the understanding of the basic types of prayer and to write our own versions of prayers that are often heard only as rote recitation. In most cases, these student-generated prayers retain the original flavor of their historical counterparts, but are infused with a playfulness and vocabulary that befits and reflects the sensibilities of sixth- through eighth-graders.

Remembering the fancy names of the types of prayer can be a challenge. After we had covered each topic, we used Story Cards to review. Story Cards are playing cards; each card has a picture of an object: beach ball, tiger, chainsaw, and so on. Rory's Story Cubes or Pictionary cards can be used in a similar fashion, or you can make your own deck of cards using the names of familiar objects.

To play, each student blindly selected three story cards from the deck. We went around the room in a circle; each person was required to make up a prayer to include one or more of the story cards in his or her hand. After the prayer was recorded on the board, the student was asked to identify the type of prayer they had created. Below is an example of part of the list our group generated; it's a ridiculous list, but the exercise is quite useful for becoming comfortable with the cadence and vocabulary of prayer.

Dear God,

Please bring me beach ball weather. Please provide elders
with scooters. Please save Peter from fiery tornadoes and send
Alison's trees a knight to protect them from any ghosts (supplications). I confess that I ran over an alien and a monster,
and I stole a set of bunny ears, all to get a pig to feed the poor
(confession and intercession—sort of). Thank you for the colorful necktie; it goes with the bunny ears that I stole from Wendy
(thanksgiving).

One of the most common complaints I hear about prayer and worship is that they are boring. For a variety of complex reasons, the language and structure of common prayer can put kids off. What follows is a primer of ways to use comics to aid in your conversations about prayer and its practice.

Case Study in Comic Prayer: Exercises and Applications

For each type of prayer discussed, I recommend following some simple steps. First, educate. Use a variety of exercises to explore, discuss, and generate prayers for use in a variety of situations and settings. Examine the origins of different types of prayer and their contexts. We looked at prayer modalities from different faith traditions (for example: prayer flags, mandalas and sand paintings, rosaries) before concentrating on the forms found in the Book of Common Prayer.

Second, create characters, considering their functions within your prayer book project. Have students imagine and record origin backstories of their characters. Where did they come from? What are their quirks, talents, and downfalls? How and why do they relate to the practice of prayer? These stories tend to be elaborate, so make sure the details get written down. You can distill the stories into useful parts later. If your kids get stuck, use a series of writing prompts to get them started (see Appendix B).

Third, focus on production and distribution. In what order will your prayers be presented, and which prayers will be accompanied by illustrations? What will your page layouts look like? Will the text be hand-written or typed on the computer? Will you use color? How many copies will you print, for what audience, and will you charge or give them away for free?

However you decide to incorporate comics into your curriculum, remember this: Kids always have something to contribute to conversations about prayer, whether or not they immediately believe it. As evidence, I offer to you Brian's comic about SaXOS, a one-eyed saxophone who prays without ceasing, and Demonic G, a malevolent character who is driven nearly mad by the constant chatter. The final panel

Brian Materne

in this humble strip indicates that regardless of the circumstances, prayer is always possible. We always have "more buttons"–and that is an important message to kids who often think they have nothing to say or that they are saying it wrong.

Each subsection of prayers in the pilot *Book of Comic Prayer* is introduced by a character or characters created by the art team. These characters reappear when clarification or additional description is necessary. What follows is an explanation of our process in creating these prayers and the cartoons that accompany them.

Pizza Be With You: Table Blessings

If your youth group regularly shares meals, the practice of saying grace is a painless way to introduce the practice of prayer outside of the sanctuary. People who eat together have a ready excuse to pray to-gether. Ask your students if they say grace when they dine with their families. Do they have a favorite prayer they remember from their childhood? Write down as many table blessings as the group comes up with. If this is not a fruitful conversation, read and discuss traditional graces in the BCP or in Julie Sevig's delightful book *Peanut Butter and Jelly Prayers*.[83] Write a group prayer and agree to use it before every youth group meal. Write new ones seasonally or to match the food being served. One of our group's favorite graces emerged during our Halloween get-together, during which we happened to be chatting about the zombie apocalypse when this emerged: "Give us this day our daily brains." Accepting and using this tongue-in-cheek treatment of the table blessing makes prayer authentic and surprising and gives kids ownership of their gratitude.

This works well with younger children, too. In our lesson about the Great Thanksgiving, we talked with our third- through fifth-grade church school class about the connection between the Eucharist and thanksgiving. We served a selection of foods to represent those that Jesus and his disciples might have had at the Last Supper in addition to bread and wine. While we snacked on Goldfish crackers, olives, cheese, and Fig Newtons, we shared some of our favorite snack items. From this list, we created a table blessing just for our class:

Thank you for cookies
And candy that's gummy,
Pizza be with us
And fajitas that are yummy;
For chocolatey things
And food from all seasons,
Lord, we give thanks
For so many reasons.

Abigail Ray and Lock Billingsley

The students then illustrated their prayer with drawings of gummy bears, pizza slices, and Hershey bars.

Collecting Prayers

After graces, we continued on to the collects, talking about the very nature of collective prayer. In the Anglican tradition, a collect literally serves to *collect* the thoughts and concerns of those assembled as well as to include those who are absent. In one exercise, we provided a template. In another, we split the kids into small groups and had the groups read together descriptions of the basic parts of a collect: address, ascription, request, consequence, and doxology. Each group completed a worksheet in which they wrote their own collect. Written to the standard "Heavenly Father" as well as to "Our Biffle God," the results are a combination of questioning, wonder, trust, and concern.

The Pew Potatoes are in charge of introducing the collect section. Representing the wide variety of personalities that attend any given church service, the Pew Potatoes range in attentiveness from highly engaged to absentmindedly holding the prayer book upside down. They are a tribute to preoccupied minds and searching souls alike. The

Brian Materne

Brian Materne

important part is that they show up week after week, demonstrating a longing for sustenance in the form of prayer, worship, and community. The Potatoes represent a cross-section of the Church; they collect the multiplicity of needs and concerns that are brought to the pews. Often bored or confused, here we see them getting a lesson on prayer from a character named Phil (pictured above).

Psalms: Praise and Pouting

Our comic prayer book uses gritty honesty and age-appropriate humor to guide readers through the reimagined Psalter and is introduced by a band of musical characters named Sam and the Personifications created by Ike and Brian. Sam is a shy-looking manga-inspired young woman accompanied by Mike, a boisterous and hard-of-hearing microphone. (Mike is a bit deaf from all of the prayers that get shouted into his head.) The band is comprised of the Carnivorous Bongo-Brothers, a self-playing banjo, guitar, and trumpet. They play a variety of music ranging from joyful, uplifting ballads to somber, lamenting dirges; their imagined playlist is derived from our initial conversation about the psalms as a collection of individual and community prayers of praise and complaint.

John Westerhoff observes that the psalms "teach us the importance of praying out of our community's experience, history, and tradition."[84] The psalms can be particularly well suited to speaking to the ever-changing moods and pressures of being a teenager. Once they understand that prayer is not the same as platitude, but is rather a relationship in which we are allowed to express ourselves, to air grievances, and to share experiences that range from great happiness and gratitude to great anger and disappointment, the psalms provide a framework by which to organize their thoughts. Last year, using a template I found online, our youth group wrote psalms that they then presented at a local interfaith Thanksgiving service.

This year, we studied a sampling of psalms with varied content, from discomfort to fear to indignation. Students were invited to rewrite these psalms as "tweets," restricting the number of letters, spaces, and punctuation to 140 characters, as allowed by the social media application, Twitter. They were encouraged to describe what was going on in each psalm using their own words. Several of the students went on to write new psalm tweets, with hashtags like #*wewantchange* and

Ike Maness, Brian Materne, and Tessa Foley

#shepherd#yes. My favorite is a simple listing of how each of five kids was feeling. It speaks to the range of emotions we bring to prayer at any given moment.

#5words

Cold. Hungry. Irritated. Tired. Fabulous.

Some kids will initially argue that the psalms have "nothing to do with" them. This apparent irrelevance switches to a cautious interest once they are told that the psalms are full of angst and angry shouting about everything from enemies and bullying to hypocrisy and deceit. This is not to say that the psalms are negative. It means that they are *real.* The psalms are the lamentations and jubilations of ordinary people living with real stressors and sadness. They are also full of surprises and rejoicing. The roller coaster ride of the psalms often echoes the experience of youth whose environments and relationships and bodies and technologies are changing at rapid rates.

Once your students are familiar with the background and structure of the psalms, they can explore further by tackling a longer-than-a-tweet version. One of the mechanisms employed in the psalms to assist in memorization is the acrostic (see Psalm 119). In the original Hebrew, each line of some psalms begins with the same letter, which then changes with each subsequent section. Writing this kind of psalm is a challenge that children of all ages can achieve with success. It is also a fine way to connect the shorthand language of texting and instant messaging with the practice of prayer.

Begin by inviting your class or group to come up with an acronym that interests them. It can be the initials of their school, church, or other organization. In our case, the kids chose "O.M.G." This works both in a large group: as kids shout out ideas, write responses on a flip chart so everyone is able to see; and in small groups: assign each group a letter and ask them to compose four to six sentences beginning with that letter. Here is one of our acrostic psalms:

Oh Lord, we worship you for all eternity;
One God guides us; you are the only Lord.
Over time, we have developed our faith;

Our God, we put our faith in you alone.
On this day, we are grateful for you and all your goodness.
Oh Lord of zestiness, we kneel at your holy feet;
On top of your world, we stand.
Many miracles have you performed;
May you continue to guide our steps towards a straight and
    steady path.
Make our walk through the challenges of this life easier;
Guide us through our busy lives.
Get us through tough times,
Giving us the will to forge on ahead.
Grateful are we for the gifts you have given us;
Gracious God, we thank you for walking with us.

The Anti-Psalm

I first encountered the term "anti-psalm" in an essay by poet Alicia Ostriker. She writes:

> The Psalms are overwhelmingly beautiful as poems. They represent the human spirit, my own spirit, in its intimate yearning for a connection with the divine Being who is the source of all being, the energy that creates and sustains the universe.[85]

They are also, grumbles Ostriker, simultaneously glorious and terrible. Anyone who reads the psalms without sensing the bitter mixed in with the sweet is not paying enough attention.

Addressed to God without the expectation of a response, the anti-psalm is a reaction to her resistance to "a God who deals cruelly with us and demands our praise."[86] Whatever your theology, being angry or disillusioned with God is a natural byproduct of an unpredictable world. "What does remain constant throughout," says Ostriker, "is faith that God exists, whether present or absent."[87] In the spirit of these observations, it is an instructive exercise in faith to compose some anti-psalms of your own. It is also a great activity to piggyback onto the psalms described in this chapter.

One way to create an anti-psalm is to identify an emotion from an existing psalm and write a rebuttal. ("'Make a joyful noise'?" "I just

failed my math exam so I'm going to throw my math book at a wall!")
Teenage angst usually provides ample subject matter for this lesson.
Another option is to write a response to a psalm from God's point of
view. In either case, inventing characters and framing the response
within the structure of a comic strip takes some of the anxiety out of
the exercise.

Gabby initially struggled with the everyday relevance of the psalms,
so when it came time to talk about anti-psalms, she chose to make a
comic about it instead of using verse. The question mark in her strip
finds psalms to be boring and inaccessible, reflecting Gabby's original
reaction. The exclamation point represents the learning and growth
that can take place over time and with increasing familiarity with any
form of prayer. The psalms still may not be Gabby's favorite subject,
but she has been able to visually demonstrate her understanding that
they can have meaning apart from their biblical context.

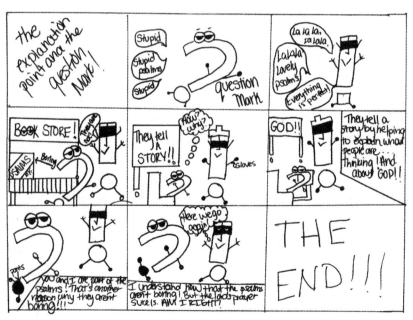

Gabrielle S.

P.O.P. Art

The prayer book actually encourages us to write our own intercessions,[88] even providing guidelines of what to include. For youth groups,
the prayers of the people are usually the easiest to compose, once kids
get past the expectation that their versions will mirror the language of
the forms in the Book of Common Prayer.

I have two particular exercises that work well and require little
preparation. The first is a play on the word "pop." Cut some pieces
of paper into thin strips and hand them out to the members of your
group. Tell the group to write their intercessions on the strips of paper
with the understanding that they will be shared with the group. Have
a box or basket of un-inflated party balloons available. Each prayer is
to be folded or rolled up and inserted into one of the balloons, which
students should then inflate and tie off. Holler, "The Lord be with
you!" They will know to shout, "And also with you!" Their cue to toss
the balloons in the air and bop them around is "Let us pray!" Once
you have batted the balloons around for a while, repeat the invoca-
tion and invite your youth to pop whichever balloon settles into their
hands. They can use a pin or paper clip, but I have found that stomp-
ing on the balloons seems to be the preferred method of popping. As
each balloon is popped, have the kids read the prayer inside. Teenagers value anonymity in their prayers, and this exercise enables them to
pray without fear of ridicule. Record all the prayers and arrange them
into a litany for your prayers of the people; let the kids determine the
response to each line.

Another simple exercise for generating intercessional prayers requires markers and a wooden tumble game like Jenga. Depending
on the size of your group give each person in your group at least one
wooden game piece. With markers, write prayers on each side of the
Jenga block. Collect all the blocks, mix them up, and have your members select a block or two. It does not matter if the block is his or hers
or belongs to someone else. Read the prayers on each block aloud,
beginning with the words, "We pray for . . . " Assemble the blocks into a
tower as the prayers are read. Close your prayer session with a game of
Jenga, inviting participants to silently pray for the people and situations

on each block they remove. When the tower falls, gather up the blocks and have your group or art team transcribe the prayers into a list. This will become the group's own Prayers of the People, which can be used in worship or other settings.

In the *Book of Comic Prayer*, Tessa's Lollipop Dragon is responsible for receiving and responding to intercessions. The "pop" in lollipop stands for "prayers of the people." The benevolent, striped dragon has colorful lollipop "scales" along her back and is fortified by prayers. A large trumpet-like tube reminiscent of something out of Dr. Seuss captures the prayers of the people. Once they are sucked into this tube, the prayers enter a complicated machine in which they are stamped on candy conversation hearts. After receiving a coating of sugary syrup, these hearts come out of the prayer press and are consumed by the Lollipop Dragon, who exhales the transformed words as a sweet, powdery, pastel dust akin to Pixy Stix. That God takes these sugary offerings and transforms them as only God can do is a given; that the prayers of the people become relevant and fun for the group is similarly transformative.

Tessa Foley

Gabrielle S. and Tessa Foley

On Comics and Confession

Author Ken Kesey observes, "The trouble with super heroes is what to do between phone booths."[89] Prayer is often what happens when we are between our own metaphorical phone booths—in those liminal spaces between the ordinary and the extraordinary. It is in these spaces that we are prone to weakness and less-than-heroic actions.

Most of us commit small daily acts of villainy, and while we may not be inherently evil, like the Joker or Lex Luthor, there are thoughts and actions that have negative consequences on our spiritual wellbeing. Using the Confession of Sin found in the Book of Common Prayer (pp. 359–360) as a reference, our youth group explored what it meant to be sinful, penitent, and ultimately, forgiven.

Writing a group confession can be challenging. On the one hand, as Margaret Guenther observes, confession requires specificity.[90] On the other, young people (indeed, any people) may be reluctant to name their sins in this public manner, so it is important to balance the conversation between generalities and specific sins. Making confession "fun" seems contradictory, but it is possible to foster an environment that is playful, meaningful, and safe by using simple props. Gather six plastic Easter eggs of different colors; tape or glue them shut. Label them as follows, placing them in a brown paper bag or other opaque container: "thought," "word," "deed," "done," "undone." Have everyone sit in a circle and invite the first person to reach into the bag and pull out an egg. For the initial round, talk about what each word means and whether it is positive, negative, neither, or both. Replacing the eggs in the bag, have each member of your group pick an egg, then provide a related example. For instance, if you select the word "undone," describe something you could have done but didn't. Why did you choose inaction? How did it make you feel? What was the result of your decision? How would you act differently if presented with a similar situation? What do you think God wanted you to do?

Record all the answers as thoroughly as possible and set them aside. This activity often needs debriefing. Now is a good time to study a variety of prayers of confession and absolution. Explore differences and similarities in wording and tone. Come back to your list of egg-generated responses and, using an existing prayer of their choice as a template, see if you can create a confession that reflects the thoughts, words, deeds, actions, and failures to act the group has identified and offer them to God. Here is our group's prayer. The response between verses is, "Help us to be better."

> God our father, forgive us for the sins we commit, both big and small; forgive us for the things we have done or failed to do.

> For the times that we have failed to help others; for the times when we have thought badly about others; for the times when we have been cruel or rude; for the times we have been willing to sacrifice others for our own needs; for the times when we have made hurtful assumptions; for the times when we have forgotten about you.

To counteract the intensity of this exercise, Lock created Fess, a top-heavy whale who wears a tool belt and muscle shirt. Fess walks upright on Flintstone-like feet; he frequently face-plants because he carries the weight of all the world's confessions in his oversized head. His diminutive companion, Phil the Gill, is a slight, lizard-like creature who wears a tiny pointed hat. A loyal and cheerful chap, Phil accompanies his giant partner like pilot fish, propping Fess up whenever the prayers become too onerous. Periodically, Fess releases the confessions via his blowhole, spraying a fine mist of absolution. (Phil carries an umbrella.)

Harold Be Thy Name

Deconstructing the Lord's Prayer can be a long and arduous process. Most of our kids know the prayer by heart, but there are those who are less familiar with it, and certainly most are unaware of what they are actually saying week after week. My goal as an advisor is to approach the prayer from a place of humor and understanding. One year,

Lock Billingsley and Brian Materne

I took the prayer apart, leaving blanks in place of the "important" words. Using this Mad Libs format, our kids (who weren't aware of what we were working on) filled in those blanks using words of their own choosing. When the rewritten Lord's Prayer was revealed, with its references to burping and robots, everyone laughed. A few were horrified. I explained that this exercise was designed to increase their familiarity with the prayer's structure and to have some fun in the process. We would not be replacing the Lord's Prayer with a random assortment of adjectives and adverbs any time soon.

This year, we turned the Lord's Prayer into a rebus. A rebus is a puzzle in which images are combined to represent words. Decoding the rebus is not always meant to be simple. In our case, each youth got a prayer book and a piece of paper, on which they were asked to draw a picture or symbol for each word in the Lord's Prayer. We reviewed all the drawings as a large group and then decided which image would be paired with each word. "Our" is an hourglass; "who" is represented by an inquisitive-looking owl. Some of the words were more difficult. What does "hallowed" look like? For "thy," should we use a chicken thigh or a human one? How do we depict words like "as," "it," and "is"?

The art team took over from there, compiling the images, which were then scanned and arranged in the proper order. The result of our rebus challenge is reprinted on the next page.

In the spirit of our struggles with the Lord's Prayer and our subsequent laughter, a fellow called Derpy oversees this section of the *Book of Comic Prayer*. Derpy the Dopey Disciple was born of frustration with the often dim-witted behavior and lack of comprehension displayed by the disciples. Derpy is no different; he says things that aren't too bright, and never seems to get things right on the first try. He is a bit like us, and he never stops trying to understand what Jesus was getting at.

Going through a prayer line-by-line and word-by-word is both instructive and challenging. Repetition breeds familiarity while dissection leads to a level of competence, each of which is necessary to understanding. When it comes to the Lord's Prayer, Derpy is a willing, if not so swift, student. Instructed by an unseen teacher, he misinterprets

Brian Materne

Lock Billingsley

at least part of each line and what results is an amusing repartee reminiscent of an Abbott and Costello skit (see previous page).

Derpy makes visible our limitations as people of faith, as well as our longing for meaningful dialogue with God through prayer.

"This I Believe": Creeds

A creed, stated simply, is a statement of belief. One approach to becoming familiar with the language of belief is an adaptation of NPR's long-running radio show *This I Believe*. Since the show's beginning in 1949, hundreds of essayists have expressed their beliefs in the form of a three-minute monologue read on the air. The program offers several helpful guidelines to composing a statement of personal belief: Tell a story. Be brief. Name your belief. Be positive. Be personal.[91] The guidelines elaborate on these simple instructions, which are available both in the book of the same title and on NPR's website.[92]

The program doesn't state what type of belief to describe. Previous essays tell stories about subjects ranging from atheism to jazz to the power of good barbecue.

Each story is creed-like in structure and tone. The very name of the radio show is creedal in nature. This I believe. I believe this. It's a great gimmick, and one that works well with young people struggling to define and articulate their beliefs about God, the Church, their surroundings, and their futures.

Our art team listened to excerpts of a few essays before identifying subjects to write about. The main criteria were that their essays had to be no more than five hundred words in length and that they had to be true. Being true is not defined as having happened exactly as described; truth, in this setting, is more about being *real*, about being true to experience, authentic, and honest.

Once their compositions were finished, the team moved on to storyboarding. Is there a clear beginning, middle, and end? What are the main elements that need to be depicted and how will you keep the story moving? Who are the main characters? What do they talk about? Using storyboard templates, the kids completed thumbnail sketches of each panel, accompanied by narration and dialogue.

Finally, we created crisp, clean comic strip versions of their stories based on their previous work. Lock's comic describes a dream he had that supported his belief in God. In the dream, Lock is sitting on his couch, minding his own business, when God appears next to him. He is unafraid because, "I knew it was God." The strip goes on to explain that, had this happened in real life, Lock would have been scared, wondering who this person was and how he had gotten into the house. It is a compelling commentary on the dual nature of God as a source of comfort and anxiety as well as our own tendency to let fear and doubt interfere with our firm belief in God's goodness.

"God is the compassion and love in all of us" and is available to everyone. This is the message of Tessa's essay and corresponding comic strip. My favorite panel shows a large billboard on which is printed, "Call 1-800-God-Now! Available 24/7!" In just a few panels, Tessa has created an effective advertising campaign whose focus is on being both the recipient and benefactor of God's love.

Sure of his beliefs but unsure where to start with his writing assignment, Ike decided to explain his beliefs about God as if he were describing them to a Martian. Pairing a deep reverence with dry wit, my co-leader Wendy invented "Super Chalice and Wonder Wafer" to illustrate her belief in the power of the Eucharist. In this strip, we are introduced to the troublesome "Unholy Molar" and its transformation by the sacrament.

We could easily spend an entire program year on the Nicene Creed, its history, and its meaning. With only two or three hours allotted for our classroom time together, I have learned to make use of the limited time creatively. For this section, we compared the Nicene Creed to the Apostles' Creed, the Maasai Creed, and even a creed of the Flying Spaghetti Monster I found on someone's blog.[93] We examined these statements of belief in terms of what they said, what they left out, and how they were structured.

For our introductory activity, I introduced them to Austin Kleon's book of poetry entitled *Newspaper Blackout*.[94] Each poem in this wonderful book was created by taking a black magic marker to an article in the *New York Times* and crossing out large areas of words. The remaining words form a story or poem and add a new element of

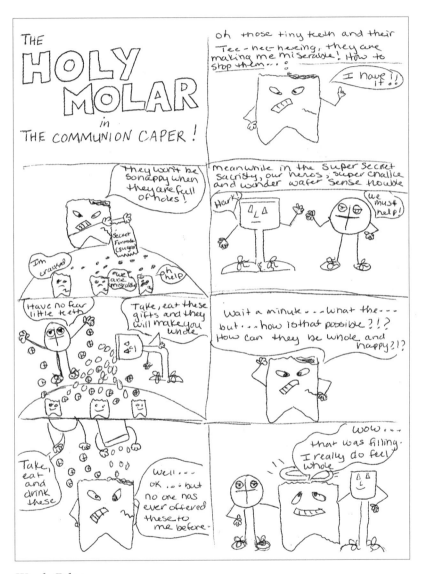

Wendy Foley

meaning to the newspaper. For our exercise, I handed out markers and copies of the Nicene Creed and asked the kids to black out any words and phrases they thought were unnecessary. The idea was to reduce the creed to its most basic form.

What resulted was a pile of blackened pages. Lucas, who, despite treating the exercise like a bit of a joke, emerged with what I find to be a most profound and succinct statement of belief. He had obliterated almost the entire creed, leaving only these few words: "Believe God, the unseen."

The following week, we continued with a more in-depth exploration of the creed. Using a list from the confirmation curriculum *Confirm not Conform*,[95] we broke the youth into small groups with the following instructions: "Write down what you believe about these concepts. Not what you think you are supposed to say, but what you actually believe to be true." The list includes doctrinal words and phrases like "heaven," "sin," "Jesus's ministry," "forgiveness," "what God does," and so on.

Coming back together, each small group appointed a spokesperson to report the most common responses. These were recorded on four sheets of flip chart paper and discussed. Again, the art team took the responses and distilled them into a representative statement of faith. When I had them read it aloud, we were all silent (which is unusual for middle schoolers!).

We believe in God, the creator of life, heaven, and earth. God watches over us, protects us, loves us, and sends us in the right direction. God created land and water, all living creatures, day and night, light and dark, and us.

We believe in Jesus, the son of God and our savior; he helps us, teaches us, and enables us to grow. Through his crucifixion he was punished and sacrificed for us. Through his death, we are freed from our sins. Through his resurrection, he was brought back to life, symbolizing our own rebirth in God's eyes. Through the bread and wine Jesus gives us a reason to believe in him.

We believe in the Holy Spirit who is active throughout the world and is inside us, part of us. The Holy Spirit looks after us so we don't suffer and guides us to make the right choices.

We believe that heaven is where everyone goes, no matter what. We believe that Jesus died for everyone–not just the "good guys." We believe in second chances.

We believe that sin is an action, thought, or word that goes against what God would want us to do. Nobody's perfect but we believe that we are worthy to be forgiven. God's forgiveness is a sign of relief and weight off our shoulders.

We believe in the Church as a place to worship and connect with God, Jesus, and the Holy Spirit.

Our group struggled for a while to come up with a character to personify the creed. One afternoon, in between mouthfuls of pudding, Gabby started describing what we came to think of as the antithesis of creedal behavior. If creeds are rigid and unquestionable, what might the opposite look like? The responses came tumbling out of the group: a girl wearing a traditional parochial school uniform, complete with plaid skirt, who rebels and questions and rails against the established system of beliefs. "Am I allowed to be the person I want to be?" she asks. "Am I allowed to believe what I want to believe? Will God believe in the person I want to be?" A fascinating conversation about rules and individuality ensued. At long last it was decided that this character should be called "Blur." It was agreed that her very features should be indistinct, signifying her uncertainty and the fluid nature of her beliefs. Her ruler-straight skirt and buttoned-up blouse are indicative of the difficulty of unflinching belief and response to confusing doctrines.

Lists of Thanksgiving

One Sunday evening, I announced that we were going to be studying and creating a Litany of Thanksgiving. "What's a litany?" they wanted to know. When I explained that a litany is essentially a list, they asked, "Why can't we just call it a *list*?"

Gabrielle S.

They were right. Sometimes we overcomplicate things, and giving thanks ought not to be a complicated endeavor. For this list of thanksgivings, we asked kids to brainstorm things for which they were thankful in various categories: people, the natural world, things that are blue, things that are tiny or giant, things that can be sensed. You can create your own categories dependent on the season, liturgical calendar, current events, or just compile a series of random items or qualities.

God of everything, today we thank you for all the good things which flow from you.

Thank you for plants and trees and animals—the deer and the ostrich, the turkey and the shark.

We thank you for the gifts of breath, love, genius, and peace; for family, friendship, and pets.

We thank you for the knowledge of people's differences, for the gift of caring about people and being cared about, and for being fascinated with ourselves and others.

We are thankful for the blue sky, the blue ocean, and the blue Tardis; for elephants, whales, black holes, and the overwhelming bigness of God.

We are thankful for finding God in the small things of life, from electrons to peanuts, from goldfish to gumballs; for those things that awaken our senses: flowers and spices, sugar and candles, popcorn and shampoo; for pie and pizza and all the foods that nourish us.

We are thankful for our lives and all the riches of creation, too many to name. *Amen.*

For this next example, each person was given an index card and invited to write three things that he or she is thankful for. The art team later collected the cards, putting the words and phrases into sentence form that can be used at any time; the response between verses is "Hear our prayer."

God, you are awesome, snazzy, and smart; we offer you our
    prayers of thanksgiving:
For family and good friends;
For a roof over our heads and food on our plates;
For pandas, dogs, and alpacas;
For pasta and junk food;
For youth group;
For the life and unconditional love we have received;
And for all blessings, big and small, Lord, we give you thanks.

Prayers for Peace

Praying for peace means more than praying for an end to war and conflict. Our church school and youth group had several in-depth discussions about the meaning of peace: who is in need of it, and how one knows if one has it.

In our third- through fifth-grade class, we used Isaiah's description of "peace like a river" (Isa. 66:12, NIV) to talk about peace and what it looks like, sounds like, feels like, even smells and tastes like ("pink lemonade, gummy bears, and marshmallows"). The group immediately identified the swimming pool as their image of peace. We asked, "What is the difference between a peaceful pool and a non-peaceful pool?" Some responses were predictable: a peaceful pool is calm, with no splashing, and is a refreshing temperature. They used words like "churning" and "mucky" to describe a pool that is not peaceful. There was some disagreement about whether a pool could be peaceful when shared with other people; the group favored a small gathering of friends over a large number of people crowding the space. During the second session, the class wrote and illustrated the following "Peace like a Swimming Pool" prayer.

Dear God, let there be peace in our pool. May our pool be beautifully colored, relaxing, and surrounded by trees, grass, flowers, and friends.

Where there is muckiness, let it become clean. Where things are rough, let them be smooth. Where there are tidal waves, let there be calm. Where there is lots of noise, may it be quiet. Where there is pain, comfort. Where there is danger, lifeguards. Where there is rain, may there be sun and rainbows. Where there is splashing, stillness. Where there are mean people, let there be kindness. Where people feel like they are drowning, may you help them float.

This super-awesome pool is the best pool in the world and we want it forever and ever and ever. *Amen.*

A Sampling of Seasonal Activities

The holidays offer cartoonists and illustrators the opportunity to observe special occasions and to celebrate in their own style. Some holiday offerings are cynical, others devout, still others are zany or ir-reverent. In each case, cartoons about elements of the liturgical year–whether intentional or not–give us a novel lens through which to view our holiday traditions and beliefs and to explore those that differ from our own. Consider using the medium of comic art to supplement the activities you do throughout the church year. The simple exercises that follow are just a few ideas for you to use with your church school or youth group.

Advent

For Advent, create a comic calendar to count down the days leading up to Christmas. Incorporate the symbols associated with the Jesse Tree. You can find a complete list online, but items include a ladder, a rainbow, grapes, wheat, a lion and a lamb, a cross, a star, an angel. Draw these objects as cartoon characters: the ladder might be wearing shoes, for example, and the grapes might have individual faces. Pair each of these images with a corresponding passage from Scripture.

It has become trendy in the past fifteen years or so to observe the Feast of St. Nicholas (December 6). Our church school children leave their shoes on the altar, to be filled with candy and toys while the kids are in the great hall making a variety of crafts. An easy way to get your older youth involved in this celebration is to create eight-panel mini-comics to put in the younger kids' shoes and boots. You might start with a spin on a familiar quote like "Twas the night before Advent . . . " and build your story from there, using elements from the legend as well as how your particular community celebrates.

Christmas

To bridge the divide between the over-the-top attention given to Christ-mas and the often-overlooked celebration of the Epiphany, I suggest a group comic project based on re-envisioning the popular song "The Twelve Days of Christmas." Create two versions, one in which your students recount the gifts God has given to them (rather than "my true love") and another in which they ponder which gifts they would bring to the Christ child. Write and illustrate the lyrics in cartoons. This is an activity that can be used with older children as well as with youth, and is an entertaining way to reframe the nature and value of gift giving.

Lent

It is a common Lenten practice to "give something up"; the items or habits chosen often make for interesting conversation. One way to incorporate this mindful restraint into your curriculum of text and images is to ask some hypothetical questions: If you were a superhero, what power would you give up for Lent? How would your characters compensate for their loss of power? Would they have to ask for help and/or work together with others to reach their goals? Or would they turn against one another to compete for resources? What did the disciples give up to follow Jesus? What did Jesus sacrifice for his followers? Write a comic about one or more of your answers.

Easter

Organize an Easter egg hunt for your comic-making children and youth. Purchase a bag of plastic eggs and place inside of each one a slip of paper that has one of the following prompts written on it: passage or character from the Gospels; part of speech (noun, verb, adjective); character; line from a familiar Easter hymn; secular Easter items (bunny, jelly beans, plastic "grass"), and a descriptor (funny, sad, angry, surprised, etc.). Add other prompts of your own choosing. Distribute the eggs to your kids; tell them to pair up with someone that has the same color egg. They must work with each other to make an Easter comic strip using the criteria inside their eggs.

Pentecost

For Pentecost, read and discuss various accounts of the Holy Spirit as found in the New Testament. See if the group can come up with a working definition of the Spirit and create a character (or characters) that embodies this definition. Build a story around the theme of the Holy Spirit at work in modern times. What would happen if the Holy Spirit appeared today? What would that look like and how might people react? Would the Spirit appear as a dove, or flames, or in some other form, like a text message, TV commercial, or a rap song? When have the members of the group experienced the presence of the Holy Spirit in their lives? Have them make mini-comics about those experiences.

Putting It All Together

One of the most powerful worship services I have experienced took place during a summer class in seminary. Instructor Ellen Oak randomly assigned each of us a partner and a part of the order of worship, including the psalm and prayers of the people. We were told that we could use any materials we had generated during the course of the weeklong seminars, but would not be able to use a Bible, prayer book, or hymnal. She gave each group fifteen or twenty minutes to work on their section, then brought us together in a circle. The resulting, nearly impromptu, worship was a blend of visual art, poetry, song, and movement.

Creating a brief, improv-style prayer service is a perfect culminating event for your youth group. If you have been studying prayer and making comics for any length of time, the kids will have plenty of materials to work with. If not, make available a variety of items, including basic art materials, party supplies like balloons and streamers, paper and pens, and miscellaneous props (Godly Play figures, candles, a cross, musical instruments, and so on), perhaps from your Sunday school classrooms. Pair up your students and assign each pair a portion of a familiar worship service. These might include a call to worship, psalm, intercessions, Bible story, song, and some form of homily or witness. Twenty minutes should be ample time for them to get over their initial horror and come up with a contribution. Light a candle or ring a bell to signal the start of your worship and let the kids do their thing, providing gentle encouragement if necessary, but otherwise participating without judgment or correction. Invariably, someone will be unable to control the nervous giggles. That's OK! In my experience, you will be amazed and humbled by the combination of depth and playfulness that your group will demonstrate.

CHAPTER 8

Thinking Outside the Book

Interdisciplinary Applications

We're gonna need more than costumes.

—*William Kaplan (Earth-616)*[96]

The creative breadth of comics is about as unlimited as the practice of prayer itself. That said, using comics in conjunction with other visual, literary, and digital art forms both enrich and inform your book or strip. This approach is also likely to appeal to a wider variety of students with a wider range of learning styles, attention spans, and comfort zones. Try combining various modalities with each other, or incorporate your own specialty.

Manga

No book about comics and their relationship to twenty-first century popular culture would be complete without a reference to the Japanese comic art form manga. Traditionally printed in black and white, most manga read back to front, right to left.

Using the manga style to illustrate stories in your classroom or youth group may require you to check out some books on how to draw manga to have as reference materials. Chances are you will have at least one person in your group who is familiar with the style and knows how to draw it. Others will have to learn the meaning of various features, such as eye shape and hairstyles, each of which serves to identify elements of a character's personality and function. Below are a few ways to incorporate manga into your program of study.

Manga Portraits

Art supply company Dick Blick offers a free download of a perfect introductory manga-drawing lesson.[97] The lesson involves the students tracing the outline of their school portraits or other large photographs. Actual facial features are replaced with manga-style hair, eyes, noses, and mouths, the shapes of which are explained in the three-page document. Finally, images are traced onto mylar sheets—plastic overhead sheets work well and are available in bulk—and painted in the manner of animation cells.

Beginning with the End

This exercise is a play on the fact that most manga read from back to front. Review the elements of Joseph Campbell's hero's journey described in chapter 4. Tell your kids that they will be writing a story starting with the conclusion and working their way back to the beginning. This is an exercise you can do in parts, assigning one group the call to adventure, another group the ordeal, and so forth.

A variation of this lesson plan is based on a short story by Neil Gaiman called "In the End," in which he rewrites the biblical creation story starting on day seven.[98] Write and illustrate a creation story from the point of view of God, starting with the Sabbath and ending with the void. Or, take another familiar story with discrete sections, such as the Triduum or the plagues, and do the same.

A third adaptation of this activity is reminiscent of a series of books that was popular when I was a young teenager. In *Choose Your Own Adventure* books, readers could change the outcome of the story by turning to different pages, each of which led to an alternate ending or plot twist. In our case today, your manga should have a clear ending and middle, with a variety of possible beginnings or origin stories. This is another opportunity for small group work, assigning each group to a different beginning.

Poetry

Cartoonist Dave Morice is undoubtedly the most well-known comic poet, who turns poems into comics with a sense of respect and humor. In a review of Morice's anthology of illustrated verse, Bruce Brooks observes that "[t]he basic effect of poetry comics is a complicated amusement somewhere between the ridiculous and the critically insightful."[99]

It is this balance between insight and silliness that we hope to achieve when introducing kids to the concept of turning their prayers into poems and their poems into comic art. The arrangement of panels, pictures, and narration has bearing on the successful reading of a comic strip in much the same way that the order and cadence of words has on how a poem is received, and how a prayer creates and communicates meaning. Cartoonist Gregory Gallant (popularly known as Seth) observes, "The condensing of real life experience into a comic page is the very essence of what making a comic is about."[100] Prayer and poetry are concentrated forms of expression in much the same way as comic strips and books are storytelling devices. Combining these three modalities makes for a multi-layered lesson plan that is both interdisciplinary and unexpected.

As with any form of praying, thinking poetically takes practice, but there are some simple and fun ways to get yourself and your students into a poetic and prayerful frame of mind.

Prayer in Seventeen Syllables

Seth asserts that reading certain comic strips is like reading haiku; there is a "specific rhythm" to how panels and dialogue are arranged in a strip.[101] The Japanese art of haiku is often the first exposure to poetry that children are given once they have outgrown nursery rhymes. The basic structure of a haiku is three lines of verse with five, seven, and five syllables, respectively. Haiku provide an opportunity to creative a poetic snapshot of a moment or experience, usually related in some way to the current season. Writing prayers in this manner is a systematic, non-threatening way to begin the practice of mindfulness, connecting everyday experience with prayer within the context of a poetic form that is both formulaic and flexible.

If writing poetry from scratch is too intimidating, practice using a set of Haikubes[102]–sixty-three word cubes plus two cubes with prompts to help get your poem started. Illustrate your completed haiku in three-panel comic strips, keeping the imagery simple and uncluttered.

Flipping Through Faith: Animation

One of my earliest memories of animation is watching Hanna-Barbera cartoons on Saturday mornings. From *Scooby Doo* and *Yogi Bear* to the *Flintstones* and *Mr. Jinx*, I was entranced by the heavy black outlines and painted backgrounds. In the fourth grade, I made my first trip to the Rhode Island School of Design (RISD) Museum of Art. While the exhibits captivated me, I was equally enthralled by the museum gift shop. There I purchased a Disney flip book. Smaller than a deck of playing cards, the full-color flip book showed a dissatisfied Donald Duck at the theater on one side and Mickey Mouse escaping from a giant on the other. The book, which lists no copyright date but is labeled simply as #90440, is sitting on the table next to me as I type this paragraph.

There is little explicit religious content in the history of mainstream animation. Religion has been seen as more or less off-limits in the industry, with the exception of the moral values implicit in many Disney movies. There are some exceptions to be found in classic Warner Brothers cartoons and in popular modern series like *The Simpsons* and *Family Guy*. Consider incorporating some basic animation into your comics curriculum and see what kind of animated theology your group can create.

For a few dollars at an arts and crafts supply store, you can get a package of blank flip books. You can also use a package of Post-It notes for an inexpensive, ready-made flip book. Once you have created a simple character, in a few steps you can set that character in motion. Starting with the last page of the book, draw your subject. Draw it darkly enough to be seen through the sheet directly before it, on which you will draw the same character in a slightly different position. Repeat the process until you reach the top page of your booklet. Give it a flip and see how it works; make adjustments to your drawings if something moves too quickly or not quickly enough. Visit http://www.wikihow.com/Make-a-Flipbook for more detailed instructions.

Photography

As discussed in chapter 6, we incorporated photography into our Mr. Peace comic book project by inviting the congregation to travel with laminated copies of our star character. "Flat Freddy" was photographed all over the country. This is an easy and inexpensive way to get people of all ages interested in your project. When your group has designed a character—it can be a superhero, but it certainly doesn't have to be—photocopy it on white cardstock or ordinary copier paper. At your social hour, during Sunday school classes, or at some other designated time, tell parishioners that they can personalize the "flat" character with crayons, colored pencils, or markers. Once complete, laminate them using either a heat machine or self-laminating sheets (the stiffer, the better). Cut around the shape of the drawing, leaving about a quarter inch of plastic around the edges. Make the artwork big enough to be seen in a standard photograph but small enough to be carried in a purse or used as a bookmark so that people are reminded to take it along wherever they go.

Parishioners can submit photos of their new traveling companion via e-mail, social media, or by having them printed on paper. Each photo should be labeled with the contributor's name and the location of the photo. Once you have collected enough photographs, create a comic-style photo album with a travelogue theme. First, lay out your book using a desktop publishing program. Then, have your students add captions, word balloons, and any kind of story line. Is your character on vacation? On a mission trip or pilgrimage? How does he or she get around? Is he or she traveling through space? Time? Does he or she get stuck at the airport? Go swimming? The possibilities are endless and the results are often unexpected but always entertaining or educational.

For those who may not travel much, suggest they take pictures of the character at the grocery store, library, or coffee shop. For folks who do not have access to cameras, provide disposable cameras and offer to have the film developed for them. Alternatively, bring your own camera or smartphone to church with you and take photos under that person's direction: in the choir stalls, sacristy, amidst the altar flowers, and so forth. (This is a wonderful opportunity to pair a member of your youth group with an elderly person in the congregation.)

Be sure to print plenty of copies of the finished comic book, listing all the participants, most of whom will want their own copy. You may want to consider creating a digital version as well, to post on your church's website or on social media. In addition, making a slide show using parishioners' images is a fun way to show off your project at your annual meeting, back-to-school kick-off, or youth Sunday.

There are many possibilities for combining photography and comics. Here are a few additional ideas:

- Send one or more of your cartoon characters on vacation. Ask parishioners to bring postcards back from their summer travels, or have them send the cards to the church office. Scan the postcards into your computer and, using a program like Photoshop, insert pictures of your characters into the backgrounds. Your characters can simply wave, take group snapshots at the Grand Canyon, pose with Mickey Mouse at Disney World, go skiing, or lie on the beach. Make a scrapbook or travelogue using the altered postcards.

- Create a comic photo directory or yearbook for your youth group. Students can make cartoon self-portraits or draw pictures of each other. Have them write short descriptions of themselves; include signature sayings, church-related activities (acolyting, singing in the choir, etc.), and stuff they do after school. Combine with photos you have taken of the group, labeled with funny captions, word balloons, or embellished with mustaches and pop-eyes. Make copies and let the kids sign each other's yearbooks.

Webcomics

A webcomic is simply what its name implies: a comic posted on the Internet. There is a growing trend in webcomics, from posting print comics online to creating comics solely for the web. Webcomics appeal to a younger and edgier audience and their reach is wide: the typical audience for one of the leading webcomics is between one million and ten million unique browser visits per month.[103]

Publishing your print comic as a webcomic seems a logical sequence. However, maintaining a site dedicated to webcomics requires time, commitment, and expertise. As an adjunct to your comics programming, including a web version of your comic strip or book on your church's website, Facebook page, Twitter feed, or Tumblr account makes good sense. This way, you are not obligated to update content on a daily, or even weekly, basis, but you still get your work out there on the Internet.

CHAPTER 9

Zine and Unzine
An Introduction to Self-Publishing

Make your own Bible.

Select and collect all the words and sentences that in all your readings have been to you like a blast of a trumpet . . .
—Ralph Waldo Emerson[104]

"So, if we have this million-dollar superhero idea, what do we do with it?" asks Eddie Bucket of his brother, Toby. Toby proposes drawing a comic book and they each dash off for art supplies. Armed with a pile of paper and some pens, Eddie suggests that Toby start with their hero's name in "really cool letters," but Toby has other more enterprising ideas. "Are you nuts? You put 'First Issue Collector's Item' at the top."[105]

You might think that this is the dreamy objective of all amateur comic book creators, but it is more likely that most zine and underground comic artists are at it for the love of the craft and for the community it engenders. These printed works are the bailiwick of do-it-yourselfers all over the world, who toil away in attics and basement studios with copy machines, long-arm staplers, ancient typewriters, and a surfeit of ideas and hand-drawn characters, each of which is worth a million dollars in the eyes of its creator.

A zine (pronounced "zeen") is essentially a self-published magazine, usually reproduced in black and white, simply folded, or bound with string or staples. Zines smack a bit of old school newspapers run off on mimeograph machines, before the advent of the digital age. I think that's what makes them so intriguing. They are a throwback to a time when print media was popular, tangible, and ephemeral. They are time-consuming yet satisfying to produce and offer original artwork and stories at a low cost to creators and consumers.

Because they are self-published and therefore not subject to editors or censors, many zines have adult themes and imagery, so it is important to screen your purchases for objectionable material before you use them in any kind of group setting. Some are educational, others are created to advance some cause; many are completely ridiculous and thoroughly entertaining. The best are thoughtfully laid out, carefully drawn by hand, and contain story lines that put a unique spin on the mundane.

When Frank Stack self-published *The Adventures of Jesus* in 1962, he created what is believed to be the first underground comic.[106] Despite this history, it can be a challenge to find zines and self-published comics with religious or spiritual themes. Because zines are part of an alternative, largely underground movement, there exist few databases or catalogs through which to search. To identify the theme of a zine, you really have to read it. There do exist online communities where one can connect with zine-makers of a like mind, such as wemakezines.com, which hosts a Christian zinesters group. Others occupy actual physical space and allow users to check out zines. Some public libraries have added zines to their collections.[107] The online craft site Etsy is a good source for clean zines and homemade comics, many of which you can preview before purchasing.

You can also find zines in many independent book stores, comic book shops, and at regional festivals dedicated to self-publishing. At a zine fest, you are likely to find lots of tables covered with photocopied, hand-folded, and cheaply priced booklets filled with poetry, photography, essays, pithy sayings, and comics. You are also apt to see curious outfits, piercings, and other wares, from stickers, patches, and buttons to large prints and silkscreened T-shirts. These do-it-yourselfers and their fans constitute a culture of art and ideas combined with thrift and ingenuity.

Basement Comics

Eddie and Toby Bucket aren't the only ones interested in self-published comics. In a *Peanuts* strip, Rerun, Linus and Lucy's younger brother, is supposed to be drawing flowers in art class. Instead, he is drawing cartoon characters. "I'm into basement comics," he announces. "Underground," corrects his classmate. "Whatever," says Rerun, turning his attention back to his drawing, much to his teacher's obvious disapproval.[108]

According to Julie Bartel, the "powerful concept at the core of zine culture [is] that anyone has the ability and everyone has the right to create meaningful content."[109] The best way to create and circulate comics and zines with a particular message is to start within your own community. Your youth group is a great place to begin, especially if you have already incorporated comics into your curriculum. Comics and zines go hand in hand, and adding a creative or expository writing element (or any number of other media, including poetry and collage) can add both depth and scope to your product and broaden your participants and audience.

The paradox of the zine is that while zines are generally written by one person, "the distinguishing feature of zine culture is that it is participatory: in order to be part of the culture, one must participate."[110] A group zine-making effort can result in a terrific product. To shift from a focus merely on comics and towards more of a zine product, first supplement your art team with kids who have an interest in writing. Their enthusiasm will help jumpstart the interest of other members who may be intimidated or think they have nothing to say. You can use many of the writing prompts and discussion questions throughout this book to get kids writing about topics that are both meaningful to them and relevant to their audience.

I always encourage folks to start slow and build on the strengths and interests of their particular group. Perhaps your parish administrator would allow you to add a zine-style supplement to your monthly newsletter. You might try adding a comic or short poem to the service bulletin, perhaps for a youth Sunday. Then you might move on to producing a full-fledged, multiple-page zine to promote an event or to sell as a fundraiser.

A Few Exercises to Help Get You Started

Progressive Writing

This is a writing exercise that is very much like musical chairs. Distribute paper and pencils to your students, who should be seated at tables in a square or circle. Ask the group for a topic, or have some pre-written topics in a hat and let a student select one.

Explain that you will play some music; while the music plays, participants are to write as much as they can about the topic, in story form. Spelling and punctuation don't matter at this point. When the music stops (at an arbitrary interval, determined by whoever has the CD player or iPod), students put their pencils down and pass their papers to the person to their right. That person is given a few minutes to read the story; when the music resumes, they are to continue the story, picking up where their predecessor left off. Continue for as many rounds as makes sense for the size of your group. (For an added touch, use compilations such as *The Carl Stalling Project: Music From Warner Bros. Cartoons*, MCA's *Saturday Morning: Cartoon's Greatest Hits* and Vince Guaraldi's *Peanuts Greatest Hits*.) Read some of the stories aloud; edit the most popular ones for inclusion in your zine. You might wish to illustrate a story or two, as well.

Make Your Own Bible

The quote by Ralph Waldo Emerson at the beginning of this chapter seems ready-made for a zine project. Thomas Jefferson rather famously chopped out all the passages from the Bible that he deemed unnecessary, creating his own version of the Holy Scriptures. While I do not recommend this extreme (and frankly, ill-informed) approach, there is something here worth exploring. What passage or story from the Bible resonates with your youth? What are the sources from which your group draws inspiration, guidance, and information? In what ways do these sources agree? Disagree? Through drawing, cartooning, and writing, invite your group to articulate their beliefs, doubts, and source material for each. This is a great exercise with which to start off your program year, especially if it is your practice to identify group norms with your youth (or any group). Perhaps your zine project will be a sort of student handbook, the first section of which is your group norms, like the Ten Commandments of acceptable behavior. The next steps would be to create an opening or closing prayer for youth gatherings, grace for meals, and so on; in effect, creating a combination prayer book and Bible in zine form.

"What's the Big Idea?"

There is a terrific list of zine ideas in Todd and Watson's book *Whacha Mean, What's A Zine?* The list offers thirty-one topics, most of which are age-appropriate; they range from a mini-manifesto about something you care about to reproducing found pieces of paper like receipts and shopping lists.[111] You might have a fun time generating your own list of things to write about: the contents of your locker, your favorite stained glass window in church, bad autocorrects on your phone, what you would say if you were in the pulpit on a Sunday morning. The possibilities are endless.

The book also happens to be a very helpful guide to different ways of folding and binding homemade booklets, copier tricks, and tips for circulating your zines. Appendix B includes a list of superhero-related story starters that are useful to comic, zine, and combined projects alike.

The Thirty-Minute Zine

This idea, borrowed from Steven Svymbersky's booklet *So, You Want to Start a Zine?*,[112] is another exercise in timed writing. It is great as a warm-up. Pass out paper, pencils, and additional supplies such as glue sticks, scissors, old magazines (for collaging), rulers, rubber stamps, and stencils. Instruct students to keep a half-inch border around the edges of their papers, which should be the size of a piece of standard copy paper folded in half the short way. This will ensure that the photocopier doesn't cut off any of their work. Allow participants to choose a topic to address and tell them they may illustrate their essay, poem, or story however they like. Give them thirty minutes (or more, depending on the amount of time you have allotted for your meeting) to write, and set a timer. Combine their contributions into a booklet (pages must be in multiples of four, including the cover with title), make copies, and encourage students to present what they have written to the group.

Group Zine

If zines are created within a context that is "active and participatory, with little separation between performer and audience,"[113] it stands to reason that a faith community presents a tremendous opportunity to bring zines aboveground. Consider making a parish zine, spearheaded and compiled by your youth group or confirmation class. Invite members of your congregation to contribute artwork and written materials. Come up with a list of questions related to your theme or topic and have youth group members interview their peers as well as elders. Have a contest to determine the name of the publication. With prizes! If you don't have regular or reliable access to a copier, ask your local print shop if they might underwrite your project in exchange for acknowledgment or a small ad. This takes some organization, but is a simple project that can showcase the interests and talents of your entire church community.

CHAPTER 10

Comic Book Grading

Evaluating Success

> An artist cannot fail. It is a success just to be one.
>
> —*Charles Horton Cooley*[114]

Evaluation is typically seen as something to be done after an event or program has ended. It is really an ongoing process that evolves as new knowledge and skills are acquired and as ideas emerge. Any creative endeavor undertaken within the context of an educational or spiritual system is, by nature, a paradox. It is essential to set reasonable deadlines and expectations in order to achieve the desired outcome and meet the requirements of your program. However, allowing room for creativity to break in and rearrange your plans is equally important. With these factors in mind, I've included some helpful questions to consider *before* you implement a program of comic-making (or any community arts project). These questions will inform the ways in which you evaluate your program as it gets underway, and will shape how you perceive and measure the project's results.

- How will the process and product benefit your community? Will it enhance understanding of your church's identity or mission statement? Will it be visually appealing? Will your audience "get it"?

- How might you present the project/proposal to your congregation? Is there buy-in? How will the project fit in with other ongoing or seasonal programs?

- Can you engage the entire congregation? Can children and youth participate? Is this something to incorporate into your existing curriculum, or it supplemental?

- What part can your congregation play in completing this piece? What resources do you have? Are there local artists you could engage?

- Are there ways to include other churches, synagogues, or community groups in your project?

- What will materials cost and how will they be paid for?

- How will the process and/or product function? What are the liturgical, educational, devotional, ecumenical, or social aspects of the project?

- Where will the work take place? Do you have dedicated (safe, secure) space to store materials, equipment, and to hold meetings or workshops?

Understanding It

Two comic strips illustrate the difficulty of evaluating art. The first is a *Far Side* cartoon in which a young Pablo Picasso comes home with a report card showing an "F" in art. We can infer that he has drawn a portrait with the features in the "wrong" places. His mother, indignant, huffs that she is going to march down to the school and meet with Pablo's teacher "face-to-face." The punch line is, of course, that Pablo's drawing has obviously captured the precise way that his family's Cubist faces are configured.[115]

In one *Calvin and Hobbes* strip, Calvin is irate when his teacher accuses him of not taking his art assignment seriously. Fist clenched in protest, Calvin hollers, "Who set Miss Wormwood up as an arbiter of aesthetics, anyway?" Hobbes identifies the subject of Calvin's objectionable drawing as a stegosaurus in a rocket ship. "See?" shouts Calvin. "You understood it!"[116]

How important is your audience's ability to understand your work? If a desire to encounter and glorify God through the ritual of making art is at the core of participatory aesthetics, what then should be made of artistic proficiency? Visual art complements other elements of prayer and worship when it reflects and communicates the shared beliefs of those producing it. When art is created in a community setting, the contributors' level of skill and commitment need also be taken into account for practical reasons, such as familiarity with materials and how much instruction is necessary.

The importance of making bold efforts to accommodate and encourage anyone who expresses and interest in participating, however apprehensive, cannot be overstated. An individual who is uncomfortable with drawing may be able to contribute in other ways. They might assist with computer formatting, collating copies, scanning images, writing dialogue, or any number of tasks associated with the successful implementation of a group effort. Those who participate in any aspect of the project must do so with a certain amount of humility, sincerity and wonder, out of a desire to connect with and serve God and invite others into the experience. Those who act as observers (like those who read and purchase our comics), must be enabled to appreciate both process and product, interpreting and responding to the artwork in a way that raises awareness of the Holy. When these criteria are met, deeper and more religious experiences–and relationships–ought naturally to follow.

Approaches to Assessment

In the world of comic book collecting, evaluation is all about grading. In this system, there is a direct correlation between condition, rarity, desirability, and the monetary value of any given comic book. A combination of factors affects any comic's value.

In the case of using comics as tools that foster learning, communication, and creativity, the focus is less on product than on process. A comic need not be "near mint" in order to be of value. Here, you might apply an arts integration model to evaluate the success of your endeavors. The arts integration rubric emphasizes content, process, and product, and offers a self-assessment tool that covers various areas including the creative process, learning environment, foundational knowledge, strategies for engagement, and reflection.[117] This model, while valuing the product, is more interested in the processes of collaboration, engagement, insight, and integrity. It asks such questions as: Do students respect the materials, environment, themselves, and other participants? Do they come up with original ideas? Do they take creative risks? Can they work both independently and as a team?

Similarly, comics and literacy guru Michael Bitz provides a rubric for assessment that measures six areas of performance: character development, settings and backgrounds, plot design, writing mechanics, overall performance, and group participation.[118] This is an objective approach informed by teaching standards and performance reviews and is a useful tool especially if your program is in any way grant-funded or part of a donor-driven initiative.

Another approach to assessment—and I recommend combining elements from a variety of techniques and philosophies—comes from a web article by Aaron Todd called "10 Questions Jesus would use to Evaluate a Ministry." Many are useful for our purposes and all consider the spiritual foundations and motivations of our teaching. The questions explore what we've earlier referred to as "sanctifying the ordinary": "Are we creating opportunities for folks to bridge connections between what happens at work, school, and the soccer field and what God is up to in the world?" "Are we making available a safe environment in which to explore, grow, and make mistakes?" And, perhaps most importantly, "How will this help God be known more fully . . . ?"[119]

Forward Movement's *Confirm not Conform* curriculum offers a variety of tips for evaluating spiritual formation programs. Of the fourteen suggestions offered by CnC's Laura Darling, three are of particular significance. First, figure out what it is you are trying to find out by your evaluations. Second, "leave room for unexpected responses!" Third, use the information you gather.[120] There is nothing more irritating to respondents than being asked for feedback and then finding that you have failed to use it in any constructive or discernible way.

The Hero's Journey

I like to come back to Joseph Campbell's model when it comes to evaluation because in many ways, my students' stories of heroes parallel their own journey through the creative process. Answering questions related to the journey can be a fun and pain-free way to initiate evaluation. Evaluation journeys *with* the student through the following areas:

- **Everyday life**–Where were you when you started this program? What were your expectations? Did you set goals? What were they?

- **Call to adventure**–What challenges did you encounter as part of the program? In what ways did you experience wonder? Were you ever tempted to quit?

- **Test of worth**–How did you feel about the characters you created? Are you satisfied with the work you did? How could you have told their stories differently?

- **Victory**–What helped you to keep going on the project when you felt you didn't have any ideas, or that your drawings weren't good enough? Are you proud of the final product? Did your participation change or deepen your beliefs?

- **Blessing**–How has your participation encouraged or informed others? What kind of friendships do you have now that you didn't at the beginning? Did you strengthen your relationship to the larger community? How did this project enable you to share yourself with or give back to others?

Back to the Three Rs

This final series of questions brings us full circle to the chapter on origin stories and to a *Peanuts* cartoon in which Sally struggles to remember her memory verse from Sunday school. "Maybe it was something Moses said, or something from the Book of Reevaluation," she tells Charlie Brown.[121] Those are pretty far apart and, one might imagine, difficult to get mixed up. However, Sally is onto something. The earliest steps in a project relate to the most recent ones and, as such, we are constantly reevaluating our learning objectives, outcomes, and the ever-changing needs and concerns of the community. I propose a method of evaluation based on the "three revised Rs" outlined in chapter 1. Each has its own focus, but the three are interrelated and only separated here for sake of convenience.

Reach

On the surface, this is the numbers game in which vestries and parochial boards always seem to be the most interested. It is also, I suppose, the easiest to measure, by meeting deadlines and attending to observable benchmarks. While this approach is admittedly product-focused–how many participants were involved; did the program or curriculum attract new students; how many contact hours did you log with students; how many topics were covered; how many comic books were created; if the comics were sold, how much money did you make; did you make it into the local newspaper, and so on–the concept of reach can be one of greater depth. This approach considers the "products" of the creative process, both the tangible finished comic strip, book, or story as well as the intangible products derived from education, implementation, and reflection. Although it is still oriented toward content, the task of sharing stories through the comic medium is the active means to measurement.

Relevance

Whereas reach is largely about acquiring and sharing information, knowledge, and skills, that is, content, relevance is about context. If, as Pazmiño asserts, the basic goal of Christian education is to form disciples,[122] how has the process of making art empowered people to not only proclaim the glory of God but to go forth into the world to serve? One way to "measure" relevance is through self-assessment. What new attitudes, opinions, and values have students observed? Have they discovered links among prayer, worship, service, and their daily lives? How has the creation of sequential art helped develop an awareness of the holy in the midst of routine?

Relationship

Educator and author James Comer is known for his claim that "No significant learning occurs without a significant relationship."[123] If reach and relevance pertain to content and context, relationship pertains to community. Evaluation in this area asks, "What kind of relationships are being fostered between students and teachers in the process?"[124] "How has this project promoted teamwork and fostered a sense of group identity and shared experience?" "What communal functions are being served?" Is your congregation aware of and invested in the activities of your children and youth? In what ways has creating art and story led to conversation or partnership between generations? Has sharing a tangible product, that is, a comic book or strip, increased or enriched relationships within your youth group or church school program?

One of the most gratifying moments as an educator comes when your students apply your lessons to their everyday experience. You may remember Abby, the main illustrator for our Mr. Peace project. Abby is now in art school, and offers a reflection on her participation in her youth group endeavor (see next page).

Classroom Critiques

The art school "crit" can be a daunting task for both reviewer and presenter. I work primarily with middle school students who are not prepared for harsh criticism of their artwork or writing. They get this in school, and as a Christian educator, I feel it is my responsibility to build up rather than to knock down. Given, however, what we have said about evaluation and standards, the critique can be a useful tool when used properly and with compassion.

There are several main elements of a successful critique: description, analysis, interpretation, and input. When conducting a student critique, it is important to lead with the positive. This does not mean falling all over oneself to deliver praise. It simply means that the critique is intended to be both constructive and respectful. You will notice that judgment is not one of the elements. The critique is meant to be as objective as possible.

Description

This area covers subject matter, plot, and characters. What is going on in the strip? Is the writing and artwork original? Ask classmates to describe the action, the story line, and the relationship among characters. Description is concerned with content alone.

Abigail Ray

A word about originality: Most kids are creative enough to come up with their own ideas, even if these ideas fall into archetypal categories. Villains, for example, are likely to wear top hats and monocles, while heroes have capes and big muscles. Kids are also exposed to a mind-boggling number of images every day, and these occasionally find their way into their artwork. As such, try to keep up with popular culture, at least to some degree. Familiarize yourself with the shows kids are watching on television, the books they are reading for school, the video games that they are playing. You will be more likely to catch a character that resembles Gumball or looks like it was built in Minecraft or has a name from *Dr. Who*. When kids fashion their characters after a popular image, they usually do it unintentionally because the character is part of their own lived experience; something about that character is meaningful. It is important to acknowledge this reality while enabling students to create stories and characters that are uniquely their own. Encourage students to articulate what is compelling about the character they wish to emulate, then see if they can apply those characteristics in a way that is unlike anything anyone has ever seen before.

Analysis

Composition, style, and elements such as backgrounds, the use of negative space, and color are explored next. Do the story and the artwork complement each other? Analysis also deals with context. Where is the story taking place? In what time period? What else is going on around the action depicted in the comic?

Interpretation

Interpreting comics is about the relationship between the strip and the viewer. What is the mood of the strip? How does the cartoon resonate with the audience, that is, how does it relate to the viewers' personal experiences or universal metaphors?

Input

This is a category some might omit, but I think feedback and conversation are appropriate, especially in a formation setting. This is the time for peers to ask questions, to clarify concepts, and to make recommendations. Elements to consider are transitions between panels (is there enough information for the strip to make sense?), grammar, spelling, and punctuation. It is *not* the place for suggesting that a character's head is too big or that a stegosaurus in a rocket ship is not serious subject matter.

Depending on when you conduct your critique, the amount of input allowed should be adjusted. If the critique is a regular part of an ongoing process, it can be a useful tool in eliminating extra re-working at the end. If you wait until students have nearly completed their work, too much input can be a downer. Figuring out this balance is up to you as a leader.

In a faith formation setting, you might like to include a fifth category, *reverence*. This is where you unpack moral or religious subtexts and influences in the strip. How does the artist's faith inform his or her artwork or storyline? The converse of this question is also worth examining: "How does art inform faith?" Does the simple act of drawing a character talking with God or with another character about God impact how the artist talks to or about God? Can the drawing and writing themselves be acts of prayer? Has telling a Bible story or personal experience of God in the form of a comic changed the way you perceive God's presence in the world around you?

In an earlier chapter, I offered Lynda Barry's words as an invitation to "come back" to drawing, to creating, and by extension, to engaging with prayer in new ways. I have been fortunate to serve as an eyewitness to the power of using comics–simple line drawings, words in balloons–to make connections among sacred texts, history and tradition, supplications and intercessions, and the daily experiences of young people. There is fun in profundity, and within this truth comes the opportunity to combine the silly with the sacred in deeply meaningful ways.

Let us come back and draw close to the God who is the source of all our creativity.

Let Us Draw

Games and Warm-Ups

> If you want creative workers, give them enough time to play.
>
> —*John Cleese*[125]

Most people who work with children and youth already have a virtual toolbox full of ice-breakers, mixers, and team-building games that they use to start events and meetings. Many of these can be modified to suit the needs of your comic arts program, as you will have found in the pages of this book. My favorite kinds of warm-ups involve simple props that you are likely to have on hand anyway or items that can be easily borrowed or purchased.

What follows are some additional suggestions for games, warm-ups, and art or writing prompts that I have not already covered. Some are of my own devising, others I have used and adapted over the years; for the latter, I have done my best to provide the original source, although some have changed so much over the years that the original may seem unrecognizable. I encourage you to make whatever changes best suit your particular group.

Back-to-Back Drawings

The basic rules of this exercise are based on a lesson on listening skills found in the J2A portion of Leader Resources' *Journey to Adulthood* curriculum (ages twelve to fifteen). Students should pair up, sitting back-to-back. One student is given a pencil and some paper, the other a pre-printed picture of a simple geometric design. The student with the design must give verbal instructions to her partner, who must attempt to follow the directions and produce a drawing similar to the one shown. The pair reverses roles with another design, giving each member the chance to both direct and follow. Compare the "blind" drawings to the original. How accurate are they? Where did they go horribly wrong?

I like to start with one of the provided configurations of circles, triangles, and squares, then supplement these random assemblies of shapes with some basic introductory drawing lessons from books by Chris Hart or Ed Emberley. Choose drawings that use circles, lines, and other easily describable shapes to create "simple" cartoon faces, animals, and monsters.

Debrief with the questions provided in the J2A manual:

• What made this task difficult?

• Did artistic ability have anything to do with how well the drawing turned out?

• Which was more frustrating, giving the instructions or following them?[126]

Exquisite Corpses

By far, my favorite character development tool is a modification of an exercise used by the Surrealists in the early twentieth century called Exquisite Corpse. Each participant is given a piece of 8.5 x 11 drawing paper cut in half the long way. Instruct them to fold the paper into three parts. For this exercise, each person will need a partner. In the top box, each person should draw a head with a face. Suggest a variety of styles, from standard cartoony faces to space aliens. Participants then switch papers with their partners and draw, in the middle section, a torso that connects to the head. Again, encourage creativity. Are they drawing a robot? A snowman? Finally, participants exchange papers again and add what I call "a method of propulsion." I have seen everything from feet and fins to wheels and rocket blasters.

When everyone is finished, invite each pair to introduce their creature to the rest of the group. Have them describe the drawing and share one "fun fact" about their joint creation. The stories tend to tumble out. Jot down notes and be sure to congratulate them on working together to create their very own unique cartoon characters. Collect the drawings or make photocopies for the group's idea file.

Five Card Nancy

This idea generator comes from comics expert Scott McCloud; it is a "card game using cut-up panels from Ernie Bushmiller's long-running 20th Century comic strip *Nancy*." The official rules can be found on McCloud's website,[127] and involve making a deck of cards out of old comic strip panels. Each player gets five cards; players take turns placing cards in an order that is deemed acceptable by the group. The result of the game is a collaborative comic strip that tells a unique story panel by seemingly unrelated panel.

Pick a Card, Any Card

Get a set of Apples to Apples game cards, separating the green adjective cards from the red subject cards. Add cards or playing pieces from other games like Pictureka, Spot It, Clue, or Monopoly, keeping them in their own respective piles. Have participants choose one card or item from each pile and create a superhero or villain scenario using at least two of the cards. For example, from the Apples to Apples pile, you draw "Underwater" and "Banjo." Your Pictureka card features a burglar fleeing from the bank he has just robbed. You also select the candlestick game piece. In the burglar's bag is a single brass candlestick he has stolen from the bank vault. He uses the lone candle to see in the dark. You introduce a vigilante super-banjo that chases the crook into the ocean. The seawater extinguishes the candles and the burglar is left treading water in the dark. The banjo waits on the shore, patiently strumming the same tune over and over, until the burglar goes crazy and surrenders. It's a ridiculous and challenging exercise, but you might just find the seed of a storyline in one or more of the players' inventions.

Six Parts in Search of a Character

All you need for this drawing warm-up is some paper, pencils or markers, and a six-sided die. (I like to use a giant die; you can often find these in novelty shops, or buy a pair of fuzzy dice and cut them apart.) The idea is to create a character in six easy steps; the rules are very similar to those of the kids' game Cootie. Participants race to complete a character, although the object is really to continue to play until everyone has put all the parts together. Taking turns, roll the die. The number corresponds to an item on a parts list. For example:

Roll 1–Draw a head and face

Roll 2–Draw a torso

Roll 3–Draw arms and hands

Roll 4–Draw legs and feet

Roll 5–Draw an accessory (hat, mustache, etc.)

Roll 6–Draw a word balloon

Because students will usually be forced to create their character in random order, this exercise yields some interesting proportions and creative solutions to design problems.

30 Circles

Like many of the warm-up activities in this book, this one has a three-minute time limit. It was developed by Bob McKim and requires a sheet of ordinary copy paper that has thirty circles drawn on it (you can download a template online).[128] Each participant needs a copy and a pencil. They are to convert the circles to as many items as possible within the time allotted. At first, this is easy; you will see smiley faces, baseballs, and pizzas. In time, however, students will be forced to "think outside the circle," at which point bicycles, bottle caps, eyeballs, and all manner of objects emerge. There is no "winner" of this game, unless you wish to give that honor to the person who has filled in the most circles at the end of three minutes.

Super Snacks

In the late '70s and early '80s, Hostess ran an ad campaign in Marvel, DC, Gold Key, Archie, and Harvey comics. The advertisements pitted comic book characters like Aquaman, Casper, and Wonder Woman against foes with nefarious plots. For example, the Penguin seeks to control Gotham City by hoarding Twinkies. In each case, our heroes use Hostess snacks to defeat their enemies and restore peace. The ads are ridiculous and wonderful, and are the basis for this writing and drawing exercise, which can be done individually or as a group.

Identify candy or other snack items that are currently trendy or popular with your kids. Conversely, come up with a snack that is almost universally detested and never purchased–like corn nuts. Who eats corn nuts? Anyway, once your kids have accomplished this task, have them create short comics, no longer than six or seven panels, in which his or her snack item saves the day. The snack can be anything from a sugary breakfast cereal to gummy worms. At least one panel should be dedicated to advertising their product. Hint: Be sure to bring samples of their chosen snacks to your next gathering.

Outside the Lines

For this plot-development exercise, you will need a variety of store-bought coloring books. I like the kind you can buy at the dollar store because they tend to feature generic characters (as opposed to Disney or Marvel). Look for books with as little storytelling as possible. Students can work alone or in pairs. The object is simple: Starting with the first picture in the coloring book, write a story that continues through the end of the book. Each page needs just a sentence or two. Students can also draw in new characters and backgrounds as they go along. Use the stories as springboards for comic book ideas. This works as a group activity with older elementary students as well. Hint: Kids of all ages like to color. Your teenagers probably do, too, although it is unlikely they will admit it . . . let them color once they have finished their stories or you have reached a stopping point.

Caption Contest

Every week, *The New Yorker* magazine prints a black and white cartoon on the last page of the current issue. Readers supply potential captions and the top three are printed in the magazine. For this exercise, gather a pile of "blank" *New Yorker* cartoons or create your own. For the latter option, have students draw single panel gag comics in need of captions. Coming up with suitable captions can be done in a group as a brainstorming session or individually as a contest. Students submit their captions and the class votes on the winner. This is a really simple way to get kids (or adults) thinking about the process of pairing humor with images. It is also a good way to practice paring down stories into their most fundamental elements—a skill that is vital to the creation of captions and dialogue that work.

The Versus Verses

The credit for this exercise goes to webcomics artist T. Campbell. It "takes two pop culture characters or elements that happen to sound alike and puts them in a rhyming duel."[129] Some examples include pairing zombie brains with candy canes; Dr. Seuss with Mother Goose; prayer with double-dog-dare; Steven Universe with Imperious Curse. You get the idea. The two items engage in a rhyming duel, with each consecutive sentence getting progressively sillier. This works well in pairs but can also be used as an individual cartooning or writing prompt. This is a good exercise to use when beginning your unit on prayer and poetry.

Bubblegum Comics

Since the 1950s, the sweet pink blocks of Bazooka bubblegum have been accompanied by tiny comic strips featuring Bazooka Joe and his motley cast of friends. As a kid, I thumbtacked these comics to the bulletin board in my clubhouse and saved duplicates to mail in to get free stuff like baseball pennants and secret decoder rings. For this warm-up, cut paper into two- or three-inch squares. Challenge your students to create tiny comics using a three-to-five-panel format. They can illustrate a knock-knock joke, funny story, or riddle. For an added twist, do timed drawings. Give kids three minutes to make as many comics as they can. The winner gets a bucket of Bazooka to share with the group.

APPENDIX B

Story Starters

Snoopy sits on top of his doghouse, agonizing over his typewriter. Droplets of sweat fly from his face. Finally, he is inspired. "The," he types. With a look of self-satisfaction, he declares that "A good writer will sometimes search hours for just the right word!"[130]

Getting started is often the hardest part of any creative endeavor. The middle section of the story may appear before the introduction or conclusion; you may think of a great name for a character without having a single clue about his exploits. While there is a need for a certain degree of structure in any formation program, there is a greater need for flexibility, versatility, and a little bit of faith. As with prayer, we may think we know the desired end result, but God may have other ideas. It is our responsibility to remain open to the movement of the Holy Spirit or, if you prefer a more secular term, the muse. (I believe they are the same thing.)

None of this is to say you should be wishy-washy about your goals, expectations, or "production schedule." What you should bear in mind is that creativity ebbs and flows, and that there are ways to jumpstart the process when it is lagging and enhance it when it isn't. To that end, here are a number of writing prompts you can offer to your students. These are best used as timed exercises—invite students to select any prompt they feel drawn to (or, write each prompt on a slip of paper, put them in a "thinking cap," and let students choose a prompt at random) and write for three minutes. Use the following sentence fragments to start a story.

- Thou shalt not . . .

- Here I come to save the . . .

- Don't be afraid, from now on you will be . . .

- The kingdom of God is like . . .

- Look, up in the sky, it's a . . .

- I'm here to fight for truth, justice, and . . .

- The Lord is my . . .

- With great power comes great . . .

- There's no need to fear . . .

- A hero can be anyone, even . . .

- Teenie Weenie Magic Beany . . .

- In brightest day, in blackest night . . .

Writing prompts courtesy of: God, Mighty Mouse, Jesus, Superman, King David, Spider-Man, Underdog, Batman, Jughead, and Green Lantern.

24-Hour
Comics Retreat

Every October, a phenomenon called "24-Hour Comics Day" induces budding cartoonists and comics masters alike to challenge themselves to start and finish an original comic in a one-day period. Originally conceived by cartoonist and author Scott McCloud, the event was formally recognized in 2004 and has inspired thousands of participants over the past decade.

The official "rules" of this rather crazy event require artists to complete twenty-four pages during the twenty-four-hour challenge. One way for a youth group to participate in a more manageable fashion is to organize a retreat comprised of a series of lessons and hands-on workshops; combine it with an overnight lock-in. Make sure to be clear about goals and expectations, at the same time building in fun games and unexpected twists, like serving Froot Loops and Lucky Charms for dinner while playing DVDs or streaming some classic and contemporary cartoons.

Introduce your congregation to the comic art form's connection to faith, prayer, and study. Create a sermon or presentation for use during your principal worship service and plan a small-scale comics expo for your church community. Comic conventions ("cons") celebrate the long history of the comic art form and the ongoing contribution of comics to art and culture. Make copies of everyone's comics and have them available at your primary Sunday fellowship hour; have plenty of pens for signing. Depending on the personality of your community, invite parishioners to come to church dressed as their favorite comic or cartoon characters. If you run your comic-con as a fundraiser, sell a bundle of comics for a set price (for example, twelve comics for ten dollars) to ensure that each member of your group sells equally.

If you are planning to post your group's comics on the Internet, it is important that you have kids and their parents sign release forms. You can add a clause about artwork and photographs to your existing special event consent form.

It is a good idea to prepare a list of potential comic topics ahead of time and add to them as your retreat gets underway. Write each story-starter—the zanier, the better—on a slip of paper and place them all in a basket or jar. If someone gets stuck, he or she can grab a slip at random. Some topics I've compiled over the years include:

- Villain's day off

- Sticks, stones, and rabbits

- Snowman, robot, fruit (courtesy of the Center for Cartoon Studies)

- Grape Kool-Aid Monster

- The Great Whoopee Pie Caper

- Rusty haloes and tin foil hats

Sample Agenda

Saturday

12:00–12:30	Introductions, opening prayer, and lunch
12:30–2:30	Comics 101: Heroes, Saints, and Sidekicks
2:30–2:45	Break
2:45–3:30	Power and Responsibility
3:30–5:00	Character and Plot Development
5:00–6:30	Eight-panel mini-comics
6:30–7:15	Breakfast for dinner: cereal, milk, and watching cartoons
7:15–9:00	Sermon prep
9:00–10:30	Party (music, games, snacks) and production (copy, cut, fold)
10:30–11:30	Free time
11:30	Lights out

Sunday

8:30–9:15	Breakfast: bagels, OJ, etc.
9:15–9:45	Set-up for comic-con
9:45–11:15	Church service/sermon presentation
11:15–12:00	Comic-con and clean-up

List of Illustrators

Cover images:

Holy Molar–Wendy Foley

Spike–Tessa Foley

Jedediah–Abigail Ray

Carnivorous Bongo Brother–Brian Materne

Bacon–Abigail Ray

Rita–Tessa Foley

Notes

Introduction

1. *The Book of Common Prayer* (New York: Church Hymnal Corporation, 1979), 856.
2. John H. Westerhoff, *Living Faithfully as a Prayer Book People* (Harrisburg, PA: Morehouse, 2004), 6.
3. http://episcopaldigitalnetwork.com/ens/2015/07/03/plans-to-be-created-for-prayer-book-hymnal-revision/ (accessed November 11, 2015).
4. C.S. Lewis, *Letters to Malcolm: Chiefly on Prayer* (San Diego: Harcourt Brace Jovanovich, 1964), 6.

Chapter 1: Origin Stories

5. "A Conversation with Charles Schulz," *Psychology Today* 1, no. 8 (January 1968): 21.
6. Jon Bowles, *Art and Faith: Reclaiming the Artistic Essence of the Church* (Kansas City: The House Studio, 2012), 64.
7. BCP, 819.
8. Robert W. Pazmiño, *Principles and Practices of Christian Education: An Evangelical Perspective* (Grand Rapids, MI: Baker Book House, 1992), 92.
9. Leonard Sweet, *Postmodern Pilgrims* (Nashville: Broadman and Holman, 2000), 67.
10. Michael J. Bauer, *Arts Ministry: Nurturing the Creative Life of God's People* (Grand Rapids: Wm. B. Eerdmans, 2013), 171.
11. Pazmiño, 55.
12. "Visual Literacy: What You Get Is What You See," in *Teaching Visual Literacy: Using Comic Books, Graphic Novels, Anime, Cartoons, and More to Develop Comprehension and Thinking Skills,* ed. Nancy Frey and Douglas Fisher (Thousand Oaks, CA: Corwin Press, 2008), 5.
13. Stephen Tabachnick, "A Comic-Book World," in *Graphic Novels and Comic Books*, ed. Kat Kan (New York: HH Wilson Company, 2010), 39.
14. James Bucky Carter, "Going Graphic" in *Graphic Novels and Comic Books*, ed. Kat Kan. (New York: HH Wilson Company, 2010), 82.

15. www.internetevangelismday.com/cartoon-evangelism.php (accessed December 15, 2015).

16. www.comic-con.org/about

17. www.economist.com/node/10311317 (accessed January 14, 2016).

18. www.christianuniversitiesonline.org/the-bible (accessed January 14, 2016).

19. www.comichron.com/monthlycomicsales/2015/2015-04.html (accessed January 14, 2016).

20. Darby Orcutt, "Comics and Religion: Theoretical Connections" in *Graven Images: Religion in Comic Books and Graphic Novels*, eds. A. David Lewis and Christine Hoff Kraemer (New York: Continuum International Publishing Group, 2010), 100.

21. Jack Chick, Ontario, Canada. Letter dated May 1, 2015.

22. Robert L. Short, *The Parables of Peanuts* (San Francisco: HarperSanFrancisco, 2002), 11.

23. Rob Bell, *Velvet Elvis: Repainting the Christian Faith* (Grand Rapids: Zondervan, 2005), 13.

24. Orcutt, *Graven Images,* 100.

25. Westerhoff, 58 (emphasis mine).

26. BCP, 383.

27. Bill Watterson, *The Days are Just Packed* (Kansas City: Andrews McMeel, 1993), 114.

28. Dan W. Clanton, Jr., "Cartoons and Comics," *Teaching the Bible through Popular Culture and the Arts,* Mark Roncace and Patrick Gray, eds. (Boston: Society of Biblical Literature, 2007), 329–330.

Chapter 2: Drawing Closer to God

29. "Welcome to ChI," Chaplaincy Institute for Arts and Interfaith Ministries, June 19, 2006, http://chaplaincyinstitute.org

30. Emma Silvers, "Comics, Cutouts and Commentary Combine in JCC Exhibit," August 30, 2012. www.jweekly.com/article/full/66231/comics-cutouts-and-commentary-combine-in-jcc-exhibit/

31. www.nicejewishartist.com/papertefillah/isaacb2_Paper-Tefillah-catalog.pdf

32.Lewis, 24.

33. Westerhoff, 55.

Chapter 3: Sunday Funnies

34. Russell Heddendorf, *From Faith to Fun: The Secularization of Humor* (Cambridge, UK: Lutterworth Press, 2008), 1.

35. Robert L. Short, *The Gospel According to Peanuts* (Richmond, VA: John Knox Press, 1965), 3.

36. Sybil MacBeth, *Praying in Color: Drawing a New Path to God* (Brewster, MA: Paraclete Press, 2007), 38.

37. Julia Cameron, *God is No Laughing Matter: An Artist's Observations and Objections on the Spiritual Path* (New York: Jeremy P. Tarcher, 2000), 21.

38. Short, 11.

39. Elton Trueblood, *The Humor of Christ* (New York: Harper and Row, 1964), 46.

40. Donald B. Lindsey and John Hereen, "Where the Sacred Meets the Profane: Religion in the Comic Pages" *Review of Religious Research*, vol. 34, no. 1 (September 1992): 64.

41. Hank Ketchum, *Dennis the Menace* (North America Syndicate, February 7, 2013).

42. Lindsey and Hereen, 73.

43. Rushkoff, 3.

44. Trueblood, 15.

45. David Wilkie, *Coffee with Jesus* (Downers Grove, IL: InterVarsity Press, 2013), 13.

46. Wilkie, 19.

47. Johnny Hart, *I Did It His Way: A Collection of Classic B.C. Religious Comic Strips* (Nashville: Thomas Nelson, Inc., 2009), 131.

48. http://apperson.blogspot.com/2011/05/5-questions-with-cuyler-black.html (accessed January 25, 2016).

49. Robert I. Fitzhenry, ed., *The Harper Book of Quotations* (New York: Quill/HarperResource, 1993), 223.

Chapter 4: Super Faith

50. Stan Lee, *The Generic Comic*, vol. 1, no.1 (Marvel Comics Group, April 1984): 1.

51. Greg Garrett, *Holy Superheroes: Exploring the Sacred in Comics, Graphic Novels, and Film* (Louisville: Westminster John Knox Press, 2008), 13.

52. Joseph Campbell, *The Hero with a Thousand Faces* (Princeton, NJ: Princeton University Press, 1949), 23.

53. Westerhoff, 78–97.

Chapter 5: Saints and Sidekicks

54. Joey Scarbury, vocal performance of "Believe It or Not," by Mike Post (music) and Stephen Geyer (lyrics), Elektra, 1981.

55. David Larkin, ed., *Peanuts: A Golden Celebration* (New York: HarperCollins, 1999), 194.

56. CF (Christopher Forgues), *Mothers News*, issue 40 (Providence, RI: June 2014).

57. Garrett, 29.

58. Bauer, 173.

59. Richard Thompson, *The Complete Cul de Sac, Volume 2* (Kansas City: Andrews McMeel, 2014), 231.

60. Pazmiño, 47.

61. Bill Watterson, *Attack of the Deranged Mutant Killer Monster Snow Goons* (Kansas City: Andrews McMeel, 1992), 103.

62. www.catholicnewsagency.com/news/pope-francis-sanctity-is-for-everyone-saints-are-not-supermen/, Catholic News Agency, 2013.

63. https://challenges.openideo.com/challenge/creative-confidence/ inspiration/st.-patrick-comic-book (accessed January 14, 2017).

64. Words: Lesbia Scott; Music: Grand Isle.

Chapter 6: Mr. Peace Be with You

65. Lewis Carroll, *Alice's Adventures in Wonderland and Through the Looking Glass* (New York: Signet Classic, 1960), 19.

66. http://thegreatcomicbookheroes.blogspot.com/2013/12/lynda-barrys-two-questions.html (accessed December 5, 2015).

67. Bill Watterson, *Homicidal Psycho Jungle Cat* (Kansas City: Andrews McMeel, 1994), 107.

68. *The Defenders*, vol. 1, no.#81 (Marvel Comics Group, 1979).

69. http://imgur.com/gallery/TDcDeKN (accessed December 5, 2015).

70. See www.educationworld.com/tools_templates/template_ strybrd_8panels.doc and www.printablepaper.net/category/comics for some handy examples.

71. www.huffingtonpost.com/2012/04/11/caines-arcade-9-year-old-boy-cardboard-arcade-documentary_n_1414949.html (accessed December 23, 2015).

72. http://my.smithmicro.com/manga-studio-comic-illustration-software.html

73. http://www.photoshop.com

74. Will Eisner, *The Contract with God Trilogy: Life on Dropsie Avenue* (New York: W.W. Norton, 2006), xiii.

Chapter 7: From Common to Comic

75. Scott McCloud, *Understanding Comics: The Invisible Art* (New York: HarperCollins, 1993), 92.

76. B.J. Oropeza, ed., *The Gospel According to Superheroes: Religion and Popular Culture* (New York: Peter Lang Publishing, 2005), 4.

77. Bowles, 78.

78. Will Eisner, *Comics and Sequential Art: Principles and Practices from the Legendary Cartoonist* (New York: W.W. Norton, 2008), 148.

79. www.rootsontheweb.com/Year_of_the_Bible/YotB_53_Bible_heroes_and_villains

80. *Secret Origins #6.* (DC Comics, September 1986), 3.

81. Margaret Guenther, *The Practice of Prayer* (Boston: Cowley Publications, 1998), 43.

82. Guenther, 195.

83. Julie Sevig. *Peanut Butter and Jelly Prayers* (Harrisburg, PA: Morehouse, 2007).

84. Westerhoff, 52–53.

85. Alicia Ostriker, "Psalm and Anti-Psalm: A Personal View," *The American Poetry Review* (July/August 2002): 11.

86. Ibid, 14.

87. Ibid, 11.

88. Westerhoff, 86.

89. Simcha Weinstein, *Up, Up, and Oy Vey! How Jewish History, Culture, and Values Shaped the Comic Book Superhero* (Baltimore: Leviathan Press, 2006), 47.

90. Guenther, 51–52.

91. Jay Allison and Dan Gediman, eds., *This I Believe: The Personal Philosophies of Remarkable Men and Women* (New York: Henry Holt, 2006), 272.

92. http://thisibelieve.org/guidelines/

93. http://theflyingspaghettimonster.blogspot.com/2010/12/creed-of-flying-spaghetti-monster.html

94. Austin Kleon, *Newspaper Blackout* (New York: HarperPerennial, 2010).

95. www.confirmnotconform.com

Chapter 8: Thinking Outside the Book

96. Marvel Comics, *Secret Invasion* 1, no. 2 (July 2008).

97. http://cdn.dick-blick.com/lessonplans/manga-and-me/manga-and-me-manga-and-me.pdf.

98. Neil Gaiman, *Fragile Things: Short Fictions and Wonders* (New York: Harper, 2006), 219.

99. "Review Essay" by Bruce Brooks of *Poetry Comics* by David Morice (New York: Simon & Schuster, 1982). http://ir.uiowa.edu/cgi/viewcontent.cgi?article=1072&context=ijls

100. Marc Ngui, "Poetry, Design, and Comics: An interview with SETH," *Carousel* no. 19 (Spring/Summer 2006): 20.

101. Ngui, 17.

102. Chronicle Books, 2010.

103. www.economist.com/news/christmas-specials/21568586-internet-has-unleashed-burst-cartooning-creativity-triumph-nerds

Chapter 9: Zine and Unzine

104. http://www.goodreads.com/quotes/2311-make-your-own-bible-select-and-collect-all-the-words

105. www.gocomics.com/thebuckets/2014/07/10.

106. Arie Kaplan, *From Krakow to Kryton: Jews and Comic Books* (Philadelphia: Jewish Publication Society, 2008), 137.

107. Check out www.zinebook.com/resource/libes.html for a list of libraries with zine holdings.

108. Charles M. Schulz, *Peanuts 2000* (New York: Ballantine Books, 2000), 112.

109. Julie Bartel, *From A to Zine: Building a Winning Zine Collection in your Library* (Chicago: American Library Association, 2004), 22.

110. Bartel, 5.

111. Mark Todd and Esther Pearl Watson, *Whacha Mean, What's a Zine? The Art of Making Zines and Mini-comics* (Boston: Graphia, 2006), 28–29.

112. www.zinebook.com/roll.html

113. Bill Brent and Joe Biel. *Make a Zine! When Words and Graphics Collide* (Bloomington, IN: Microcosm, 2008), 122.

Chapter 10: Comic Book Grading

114. www.brainyquote.com/quotes/quotes/c/charleshor100886.html

115. Gary Larson, *Cows of Our Planet: A Far Side Collection.* (Kansas City: Andrews McMeel, 1982), 6.

116. Bill Watterson, *Attack of the Deranged Mutant Killer Monster Snow Goons* (Kansas City: Andrews McMeel, 1992), 58.

117. artsintegration.com.

118. Michael Bitz, *When Commas Meet Kryptonite: Classroom Lessons from the Comic Book Project* (New York: Teachers College, 2010), 148.

119. www.patheos.com/blogs/faithforward/author/aarontodd/.

120. www.confirmnotconform.com/blog/7-tips-evaluating-your-spiritual-formation-program

121. Schulz, 76.

122. Pazmiño, 27.

123. Debbie Zacarian and Michael Silverstone, eds., *In It Together: How Student, Family, and Community Partnerships Advance Engagement and Achievement in the Diverse Classrooms* (Thousand Oaks, CA: Corwin, 2015) 5.

124. Pazmiño, 152.

Appendix A: Let Us Draw

125. http://www.brainyquote.com/quotes/quotes/j/johncleese133998
.html

126. LeaderReseources, J2A: Journey to Adulthood Program, part 2
(Durham, NC: St. Philip's Episcopal Church, 2009), 13.

127. http://scottmccloud.com/4-inventions/nancy/index.html

128. http://f4ward.agency/wp-content/uploads/2015/06/Untitled.jpg

129. Steve Horton and Sam Romero, *Webcomics 2.0: An Insider's
Guide to Writing, Drawing, and Promoting Your Own Webcomics*
(Boston: Course Technology, 2008), 15.

Appendix B: Story Starters

130. www.peanuts.com/comicstrips/3262047/#.VpfpxPkrLIU (accessed
January 14, 2016).